How To
GROW YOUR
INTERIOR **DESIGN** Business

Copyright © 2019 by Anita Sharma

All rights reserved.
The moral rights of the author have been asserted.

All rights reserved. No part of this book may be reproduced in any form on by an electronic or mechanical means, including information storage and retrieval systems, without permission in writing from the publisher, except by a reviewer who may quote brief passages in a review.

Table of Contents

Why You Need This Book 4

CHAPTER 1: Finding Your Place In The Interior Design Industry   8

CHAPTER 2: Branding and Positioning 16

CHAPTER 3: Competitive Analysis 27

CHAPTER 4: Narrowing Down Your Niche 36

CHAPTER 5: Identifying Your Target Clients 39

CHAPTER 6: Setting Up Your Marketing Plan 49

CHAPTER 7: Pricing Your Services for Profit 71

CHAPTER 8: Modern Web Design for Interior Designers 79

CHAPTER 9: Get Discovered with SEO 91

CHAPTER 10: Ending Notes 110

ABOUT THE AUTHOR 115

Why You Need This Book

There's never been a better time to work in the interior design industry.

Interior design continues to be a highly valuable industry across India and the United States and a most satisfying profession.

Why do I say that?

Well,
A. incomes are rising, expanding the pool of people who're looking to spend on interior design.
B. the internet and social media have made it a lot easier for designers to get in touch with clients.
C. new technology is simplifying the work of design.

Does that mean just about any interior designer can go big?

For Sure...provided they have the right guidance. I've seen countless interior design businesses fold and designers fail to prosper because they fail to market and grow their business.

And that's why I've written this book. To provide solutions that work. So that an interior designer like you can get ahead of the curve, attract more and more clients and watch your bottom line go up and up.

In writing this book, I've drawn considerably from my personal experience as a business growth consultant.

And this is not an abstract series of lectures.

This is a guide that helps you to create the best technique to grow your own interior design business.

Early in 2017, a Delhi-based interior designer - and now my close friend – Priya Choudhary contacted me through my consultation page on my website (www.searchmetry.com).

She was frantic: the problem was with her 8-month-old interior designer business, which was failing miserably despite every possible attempt to make it work. She'd gotten it up from the ground alright, but getting clients that paid enough (or getting clients at all) had turned out harder than expected.

Costs were piling – she'd already shelled out over 75,000 INR, in keeping the business afloat. The meagre revenue she'd recorded over the first 8 months was nowhere near helping the business break even or see profit.

Understandably, Priya was starting to lose morale. A lover of art and design from the moment she discovered it at age 12, she'd set out to start an interior design business that would change the game and usher in a new level of quality that she believed the Delhi scene lacked.

And like every aspiring interior designer out there, she'd read almost all the major books on the topic and followed their instructions to the dot. She'd also done a high profile online course, versed herself with the industry's latest trends and listed her business on different platforms.

Which is why she couldn't explain why her business was still failing to pick up pace.

After listening to her recount her efforts, I noticed a glaring error in her past strategies that quickly led me to the main problem.

Priya had every necessary resource for her business in place – everything except a proper marketing strategy. She later admitted to having limited knowledge on that aspect of the business, which is understandable because **a)** published resources on marketing interior design businesses aren't that common and **b)** she never thought she'd need any such strategy anyway.

Thousands of interior designers and architects continue to face a similar predicament. I've met hundreds of them personally and visited businesses with this problem. The worst part is that most designers don't realise the problem until it's too COSTLY to get back on track.

That's essentially why I set out to write this book: to help interior designers and architects understand the management and marketing sides of their businesses the easy way.

***

How Will It Help?

Packed with insider-only tips and expert advice, *How to Grow Your Interior Design Business* is a handy little guide that will help you create your own marketing strategy and provide you actionable tips to help you out of any rut you may fall into.

You'll learn everything from setting up your interior design business to safe-proofing it from industry changes, not forgetting using the various forums and platforms available to connect with your first client (and using them to get to the next client).

In short, I'll help you identify your niche, position your brand, build hype around your business and finally draw clients in, while not blowing up your budget.

I have suffixed each section with a series of takeaways at the end of each chapter, designed to keep you in the loop and give you head start towards your growth goals.

> **By the end of this book, you will be able to get your next 5 clients regardless of budget, be confident enough to charge just exactly what your services are worth and be able to grow your interior design or architect business two-fold!**

***

How Different Is This Book From Other Resources?

There is a wealth of resources out there for anyone looking to start or manage an interior design business, but the same can't be said for the availability of resources on how to **grow** an interior design or architecture business.

And while other books give you basic tips on how to operate an interior design business, *How to Grow your Interior Design Business* is aimed at helping you create your own strategy as to how your business can grow.

Fair warning though, this **isn't** a get rich quick book. The information revealed in this text will *only* help you understand what works and what doesn't, and guide you, step by step, on the journey that your interior design business has to take in order to grow.

I hope my book helps you take your business to the next level of growth.

CHAPTER 1:

Finding Your Place In The Interior Design Industry

The path to growing your interior design business starts with one step: *finding your corner in the industry*. That's about the most helpful piece of advice you'll ever get on this topic.

"*Interior designer*" might be the commonest title you'll hear being used in public and across the web, but it's a job title amalgamation.

The interior design industry, by definition, is the industry that covers everyone involved with anything related to the creation, setup and finishing of interiors.

That includes everything from floor layout designs, basement design to home furnishing, bathroom remodelling and flower arrangement. And even that's not an exhaustive list.

That's why I consider specialization to be the first step any interior designer should take.

Specialization of tasks has always been the go-to practice for humans looking for productivity since before the days of civilization. It was effective then, and it's effective now.

Many new interior designers tend to grab at every gig that crosses their path regardless of nature or skill requirement. Most believe an interior designer, like an actor and his roles, can do anything.

But even actors have ranges, not specializing can limit your business growth potential in more ways than one. I personally do not approve of this strategy.

Of course, there are many people who have successfully built up reputable design firms without specializing. They may say they don't like being limited to any niche; they love the entire spectrum of activities that fall under the moniker of 'interior design'. I've personally met some of these brilliant people.

I'll be frank here though: they are the minority. In fact, many later hire junior designers for different specialties after all.

Here's the view I offer to my clients: love as many aspects of design as you want but as far as your career is concerned, start off by choosing the one specialization you know you're really good at.

I've talked to hundreds of professional interior designers in India and in US, most of whom, upon reflecting on their work experience, agreed that my view was plausible. They'd found the benefits of specialization to far outrank those of diversification as an interior designer across their professional lives.

Interior designer vs Interior decorator

When specializing in the interior design industry, you have a few options to choose from. The most notable two are undoubtedly interior decoration and interior design. Either one can lead to a prosperous business.

But, can you differentiate them? Most people cannot. To be fair, they sound like alternate names for the same thing.

An interior designer creates the space the client requires, ensuring ventilation, ease of access, eco-friendliness and so on.

On the other hand, an interior decorator concentrates on aesthetics and furnishes the space like the client wants.

One might say an interior designer builds the place; the interior decorator embellishes it.

Of course, some designers go into decorating as well. One critical difference between the two is that being an interior designer requires specific degrees and licenses; being a decorator doesn't.

This is not to say decorators aren't important; if the designer can't adorn your room to your heart's content, a decorator is who you're going to have to call.

***

How to Identify Your Niche in the Interior Design Industry?

1. Analyse all existing options

As earlier mentioned, the interior design industry is a vast one, encompassing a range of essential activities assigned under different titles and specific to particular project types.

Finding your niche starts with identifying all the existing titles and project types available. The next step is to dissect each for its pros and cons, comparing them against those offered by other options.

Say you want to delve into interior decorating. Your options would include public places such as restaurants, cafes or diners, residential units such as homes and apartments, commercial units such as offices, and more.

You'd then proceed to analyse your compatibility with each option based on a series of factors. In some areas, only one option, such as residential spaces, is available.

2. Make an informed choice

Once you've identified all your potential options, the next step is to zero down on one or two specific ones. To do that, you need to answer specific questions such as these:

a) What are you naturally good at?
b) Which option do you really like?
c) What have you trained in?
d) What are the existing opportunities for that option around your immediate city or country?
e) How's the competition in each option?
f) Are you willing to challenge yourself?

a. What are you naturally good at?

This question should help you understand your skills and strengths which is crucial in helping you identify the right niche.

Many of my former clients had initially overlooked niches that they were naturally suited for, opting for trendier ones that appeared more profitable and respectable. Not surprisingly, most struggled with the simplest aspects of their businesses years later, despite having the necessary resources and passion to work.

So, take a good, uncompromising look at yourself. What are you naturally good at? Colour selection? Drawing? Numbers? Understanding the spirit of spaces? Note that any natural skill set is a bonus here. I've been in the presence of designers who could whip up a living space and reimagine it anew in only 8 hours and that too on a shoestring budget.

Some people are naturally inclined toward adding **'eco-friendliness'** to a room. Some people are just too good with flowers. Others are wizards with prints and fabrics. Do you identify with any of them?

Once you're done picking your strongest skills, look at the sector they are most compatible with. If, for example, you are quite good with flowers and prints selection, residential properties will be natural fit. If you have a natural affinity for luxury, luxury design is the ideal niche.

b. Which option do you really like?

Every interior designer has that aspect of design they really like, whether it's restaurant design, open space furnishing or home layout design. It's that area of design that warms your blood when you think of it.

Ask yourself, which area of interior design do I like the most? More often than not, this is easily the same area you're more likely to want to work in.

Have you always been amazed by the chic, simplistic designs of Nordic homes, or do you have an unsettling desire for reimagining your studio apartment? That can be a starting point for identifying what form of interior design you really like.

c. What have you trained in?

Training is always a big deal, whether it's from a college or an internship position. Training means you've had a chance to learn deeply and try out particular aspects of the interior design process.

Ideally, proper training accords you the opportunity to choose from any area of the design industry. In less common cases, training automatically places you in a particular sector of the design industry, especially if it was specific.

Look at your skills and qualifications. What do you know? And where can it be best applied?

d. What are the existing opportunities for that option around your immediate city or country?

Unless you have the resources required to travel away and start your business in a new city, your immediate location is where you'll be setting up and working in the foreseeable future.

So, it's important to know whether your immediate location has or will have available job opportunities for you. It doesn't make sense starting your business in a location that doesn't really need it.

e. How's the competition in each option?

I'll be frank from the start: competition isn't a bad thing, especially if it's mature and devoid of unacceptable practices. In the interior design industry, competition and the challenges it provides to designers are what propel them to do great work with every new gig.

But if there are too many designers of a similar title in your immediate area, that might not be the best option to take. Unless you can take your skills to another city, it pays to be and to offer something different.

Analyse the existing local competition in your of option of choice and see where you fit in. Is there another option with less competition? Do you see opportunities there? If yes, go right ahead and check it out.

***

The Benefits of Finding Your Niche

By now, you're probably wondering how exactly a niche benefits you. My answer? *A lot*. The interior designers I spoke to and worked with let me in on a number of benefits they accrued from sticking to one or two options rather than running with everything. I chose the best and condensed them for you here.

1. More clients in the long run

Initially, you might fear that going along with one niche leaves you with only a handful of customers, which almost never translates well for a business. In reality, having a niche gets your more clients over time as you build your expertise and grow your contacts.

Take the example of a Mumbai based regular client of mine, designer RJ Shetty, who decided to concentrate on the restaurant niche in early 2016 after two years of 'grabbing at every gig that came wildly' as long as it paid.

He admitted to me that for the first six months, business seemed slow. While the local food scene can easily be marked as alive and vibrant, new restaurants weren't opening every day in Mumbai. Those that did weren't knocking on his door either.

RJ only got to work on two small projects in the space of months: a small upstairs café above an established restaurant and a yet-to-be constructed restaurant owned by a former classmate.

The café owner wanted something unique yet no so usual, the feel of an exquisite and homey place that felt exotic but still paid homage to Mumbai. For the latter project he only served as contributor to the existing layout ideas. He didn't expect either of the projects to blow up.

When the small café did, RJ says he was hit by a sudden wave of calls. "People must have liked what they saw - and felt - while in the café" he told me. Most importantly, they wanted to get in touch with him.

Within the next 6 months, RJ had received more than 10 offers from interested people. After months of scarce work, the temptation to grab wildly at every offer was severe. "But I kept my resolve", he told me months later during a recent consultation on marketing his business.

Some offers were from home owners who wanted rooms in their houses reimagined 'with his touch'. Others weren't so inclined. He had to close his eyes and be true to his new self. Ultimately, it paid off.

The few offers he accepted during that period led to more jobs within the restaurant sector: some were re-designs of old restaurants, others involved partnerships with other designers, one even involved working on a quaint exclusive upscale restaurant in Mumbai's Borivali neighbourhood.

By the end of 2017, RJ had worked on over 20 projects, double the number he'd been lucky to land in his early years (2014-2016). The best part in all this, according to him, was the genuine feeling of loving what he was doing more and more.

By settling into one niche, he was becoming better versed with this work, and it was translating well for his final product.

The point: Sticking to a niche gets you more clients in the long run. You just have to market yourself and your business like a pro.

2. Mastery of your art

When it comes to craft, there is always preference for that one individual identified as the 'master'. The one who knows their craft inside out. The one who can be trusted. The master.

> **You don't get to become a master at your interior design or architecture craft by jumping from niche to niche and gig to gig, partially mindful of the specifics of each as you skip along.**

Mastery comes from specialization in a particular field, and that's exactly what sticking with a specific niche gives you.

RJ Shetty's example comes in handy here too. Over time, his experience in restaurant interior design over different gigs made him attractive to potential clients in search of an expert. His concentration in that field exposed him to the more mundane details other designers must skip, giving him the edge, he needed to boost his portfolio.

3. Easier target market segmentation

This resonates directly with my marketing instincts in more ways than one. Having a special niche and sticking to it makes it quite easy to identify your target market and categorise them according to their needs and interests. This is what we call **segmentation**.

With this information, you can know where your potential clients will likely to come from, what they will need from you, and what they will be able to pay. This is all golden information.

If you ask me, nothing beats having an upper hand in a business transaction. Having a segment gives you that upper hand. That way, you can know if your target market are the wealthy folks in your upscale neighbourhood or new home owners etc., and plan for them accordingly.

4. More referrals

Referrals are undoubtedly one of the main ways designers get projects in this economy. Some would argue that they also work faster than TV ads. And as revealed by interior designers themselves, being in a specific niche gets you better targeted referrals, more of which can lead to projects.

'*Targeted*' means that the referred clients are more likely to be interested in your specific area of design AND more likely to be in the segment you're targeting, having been referred by someone else. Targeted referrals are way better than random referrals.

Let's say you work in the home design niche, and have recently taken to designing for young urban couples looking for a distinctive urban taste. Your growing list of former clients may meet folks for dinner, at work or be neighbours with other people requiring services you provide.

Referrals will keep coming gradually. These are '*targeted*' referrals, because the referred clients are looking for a service that you specialize in. In other words, you're highly likely to be hired.

The same doesn't apply for other referrals, especially general ones, because half of the referred clients might be interested in gigs you aren't really invested in.

5. Better understanding of clients' needs

> **Every client is different.**
> **That might as well be an industry secret.**

Some clients will know everything about the designs they want. Others will have no clue, nodding their heads indifferently in approval as you suggest changes. Others will expect you to come with the exact solution they need.

In all these scenarios, understanding your clients' needs beforehand is paramount. Specializing in a niche gives you that benefit: over the years you learn what different clients look for and what they consider standard.

You learn how to approach different scenarios, such as the client that doesn't know what they want. All of this results in better work and better satisfied clients which as you can guess leads to more referrals and business growth.

✶ CHAPTER TAKEAWAYS ✶

✓ Interior designers are different from interior decorators. You can be **either, depending on your strengths.**

✓ You need to specialise in a particular niche as an interior designer. It gives you more expertise and an edge.

✓ Despite common belief, there's definitely lots to gain from settling into a particular niche rather than running off wildly with everything. To grow big, you have to start small.

✓ You have to understand various client segments and figure out the best bargaining approach.

CHAPTER 2:

Branding and Positioning

In this section, we cover branding and positioning, two important aspects of trying to grow your interior design business.

Branding

After choosing your niche, the next logical step is to brand yourself (or rebrand, in case you're doing this a second time) and your business. This involves some serious decision making, because the decisions you make at this stage will become permanent/remain associated with you and your business forever.

Wikipedia defines branding as *"a set of marketing and communication methods that help to distinguish a company or products from competitors, aiming to create a lasting impression in the minds of customers."* The website also defines a brand as a 'name, term, design, symbol or other feature that distinguishes an organization or product from its rivals in the eyes of the customer'.

Jeff Bezos put it better by calling a brand "what other people say about you when you're not in the room". In simpler terms, your brand is the promise you give clients about what to expect from your goods or services.

> **The idea of branding is to set you and your interior design business apart from the rest in the market in a way that makes known your values and services.**

Some interior designers don't really go the long hard way of setting up their brand. They believe a quick generic name – something like "Asher Barron, Interior Designer" – is enough for their business.

Others just go from gig to gig, retelling their names and business addresses to new clients like they're not already established. This isn't a good strategy at all. It belittles your business's growth efforts and sets you back directly by denying you a platform on which to grow your business.

The major components your brand should have:

1. Brand Identity

Also known as brand perception, this is how you want your brand to be perceived by clients and the general industry. You do this by ensuring that your brand promises clients value through its products and services in form of emotional and functional benefits.

Your identity later personifies through ad campaigns, your content and services, so it's not expected to change every two weeks. It also marks out your target audience. Brand identity is made up of the following:

- **Brand Personality/Voice**

Remember the human characteristics that we associate with people, such as class, warmth, gender and age? Give your brand some of these characteristics to give it a personality. Often, design elements such as your logo colors and slogan help express your brand's personality at first glance.

How do you like your design business to speak to clients: Modern? Young and hip? Conservative, with a touch of ageless elegance? What you pick becomes your brand's personality and will seep into your choices of clients, your choice of future hires, your future advertising campaigns and everywhere else.

- **Brand Character**

Brand character is related to how the industry perceives your brand, especially in sensitive internal matters such as integrity and trustworthiness. Does your brand deliver on its promises of quality work? This is what clients will ultimately associate with your brand.

- **Brand Culture**

A brand's culture is almost derived directly from its character and personality. In today's world, where companies are expected to have some sort of social responsibility to their immediate surroundings, the values that your brand sticks to or sides with as part of its activities also define its culture.

Values such as environmental conservation, free speech, animal rights protection etc. are good examples. It's important that your brand's culture matches your target audience's expectations to a certain level.

- **Brand Image**

In simple terms, I consider your brand's image what makes it recognizable in the market. It has everything to do with your brand's reputation, identity, character, culture and personality to customers, summed in one package.

I also consider the following to be integral parts of a brand's image:
- Logo
- Packaging
- Typography
- Slogans and taglines
- Identity Positioning

2. The Business Logo

Simply put, a brand is nothing without a logo. The logo is literally your brand's whole image, perception, culture and identity summarized into one image. A logo does brand awareness for your business even to random people that haven't heard of you before.

It's also usually the first point of contact for your potential clients before they ever decide to meet you. That alone is reason enough to go 'all-in' when working on your design business logo. I've worked with designers that didn't have a logo or see reasons to have one; most admitted that the arrangement let them down later on.

Your logo's got to be simple enough to understand, unique and uncopied for easy memorization. It's also got to be timeless enough to be relevant now and in the future and adaptable to new markets and causes without requiring unusual changes and consistent, because that's what clients expect. More importantly, it should visibly be related to your design business.

In choosing or designing a logo, I always advise my clients to check each of the areas below:

- **Design authenticity:** Because your design has got to stand out from the millions of logos already known. Whether it's **minimalistic**, **line art**, **vintage**, **hand drawn** or uses **negative space**, your logo must be new and authentic.

- **Simplicity:** As an interior designer, a simplistic logo will work just fine for you. Nothing tacky or clutter filled is recommended.

- **Flexibility:** A logo gets to be used on different materials and in different mediums, so you've got to consider one that won't present challenges when you get to that stage.

  Can it fit on a small section of a TV screen and look just as captivating as a billboard ad? Can the design be easily imprinted on different materials?

- **Color palette:** The color of a logo is everything. Experts suggest that logo color illuminates a brand's personality. Take the bright, sunny colors Fanta uses for its logo and soda varieties.

  They immediately give you a picture of what Fanta is all about. For interior designers, color has to be used in sync with outstanding design to create a memorable image.

- **Typography:** Fanta's example comes in handy here too. Its bubbly logo letters give you a feeling of fun and partying with friends. Disney's logo is another example of typography that highlights a company's brand effectively.

  Typography is associated with the fonts you use and how they appear in different mediums. I suggest you take a leaf from existing interior designers in your industry before choosing a font.

- **How memorable it is:** At the end of the day, clients and random people should be able to remember your logo from memory. It should be easy to spot and identify with your design business.

3. Designing Your Logo

You can always get your logo designed by an expert, or hire a freelancer to do it more affordably at the start. Start by creating different sketches of what you have in mind to give the designer a starting point. DO NOT try to create one yourself unless you're knowledgeable about design.

4. What works best?

From my experience working with interior designers, a simple, minimalistic logo works best for an interior designer practice. Your business's brand is best expressed through avenues like your website and your portfolio. This is what your potential clients look at first.

***

Identity Positioning

In the world of business, the importance of positioning cannot be underlooked. How you appear to potential clients matters so much – **it's the reason they may or may not hire you.**

The interior design industry, as you might already have discovered, is a cutthroat business, especially in developed countries. A client looking for a quick renovation will be met with a lot of offers, or at least have more than one designer to choose from.

Chances are that you will always be one of the many designers to choose from (unless you do your marketing right, of course). In simpler terms, you need to stand out.

Growing your interior design business requires having more than just a neat portfolio and a clichéd business name, because everyone has those two. That's what you need to position yourself differently, so that clients can notice you and identify you.

I know you're already wondering, *"What does she mean by positioning differently?"* It's a simple phrase, actually. I always ask my clients to look at how they got into the business, and how they scored their first clients.

Most, if not all, remember a similar pattern that goes somewhat like this:

Set up a business, do a couple of gigs, bag some low paying gigs here and there, do some free gigs again for referral's sake, wait on the chances of being recommended from a referral, build a portfolio and website, continue waiting for referrals, get a one-time high paying gig, slide back down to low paying gigs, and on and on and on.

It's not hard to see: this is one continuously unpromising cycle, and ultimately disappointing. But what can you pinpoint as the cause? A shallow market with no clients? Not really. A saturated market maybe. That's why they had to wait on referrals from the low paying gigs they constantly did, most of which never materialized.

One would say that this is a common problem for any starting interior designer. I do not agree. How do you explain all the other interior designers bagging regular six figure projects and building interesting brands in the same countries?

The answer is in how you position yourself. If your design business is to attract the clients it needs to grow, you'll have to step away from the crowd and the noise and stand aside.

You'll have to make clients come to you with projects, rather than have you go to them (or waiting for them to pick you out of 100 other potential picks). You'll have to offer something different without altering your craft unnecessarily.

You need to position yourself as:

a) Knowledgeable about your craft and its value.
b) Extremely professional
c) Understanding of the client's needs and willing to listen
d) A risk taker, for what you believe in
e) An achiever i.e. one who knows their capabilities and always delivers
f) One who is in control of their time and their craft

Clients may not know to look out for all these traits, but your work and your resume will reveal them over time.

So, how do you position yourself the right way?

I have a few answers to that. You'll love them all, because they're easy to try and have worked wonders for hundreds of my clients.

1. By valuing your time
2. By being extra choosy about the projects you take on
3. By proving you're an authority on matters to do with your craft
4. By maintaining 'extreme' professionalism all through
5. By delivering the best every time
6. By building strong client-designer, designer-designer relationships

1. Valuing Your Time

Every adult values their time, in an ideal world at least. You most likely do too: get to work early, finish project within deadlines, fix in some quality family time, the whole deal. That's not the kind of time valuing I'm referring to here.

My interest is directed toward the time you spend with your client, what you'd call consulting time. It's ideally the time you discuss project details, including the resources you'll need to complete it, and the costs you expect to incur.

Consultation time differs in range. For some designers, it's mere hours. For others, the process spans days. Some designers do it over Skype! What doesn't change is how important it is in setting the project on the right course.

If anything, the time you spend discussing paint colors and print finishes with your client is equally, if not more important than the actual design work you get to do.

That's what you need to value it more and show the client that you do too.

How, you might ask? **By charging for it.**

> **Create a suitable fee and mark it as a consultation fee. You can always add it to the total fee when stating your charges to a client, but remember to sing it out for clarity.**

If you're wondering why I consider it smart and professional to charge for your time, look at it this way:

Consultation time is no doubt of the utmost importance. It's where you learn everything about the project and finally determine whether you can take it on or not. Charging for it shows the client how serious you are about this project, and how invested you will be.

You don't have to tell them your whole background design process, but price alone will show how much work you put in. Most of my former clients always charged for their services in one lump fee, usually determined by the size of the project, the wealth of the client and value of the different components that make up the services.

I don't encourage this.

> **Your work has VALUE, so does your TIME.**

Charge separately for the consultation time, and also for your work, judging by its perceived value.

Perceived value can allow you to charge higher for your work, even though the sum of all its components would have resulted in a much smaller sum.

Besides, this should be another walk in the park for you. As an authority on your craft, your work is already expected to be of higher quality. And of course, in case you don't want to take on the project, you won't have wasted hours of quality time.

2. Being Choosy About Projects

I know it sounds misguided when I ask you to be picky about the projects you work on in an industry as saturated as the interior design industry. But being choosy is the best way to go. It always pays back double.

As a designer starting out and trying to make your way in the industry, doing every gig that comes your way is understandable. After all, you're trying to show your varied abilities to clients and building a portfolio for yourself.

The downside is that doing everything won't draw more clients to you. In fact, this kind of choosing will have skipping onto projects that you don't really like, straying you away from ideal projects (and sometimes better paying ones) that might come later.

Anyone's that seen a good job pass them by as they work on a smaller, less paying job knows how terrible that feels. In trying to position yourself, being choosy about the projects you work on helps you a great deal.

You make the choices, depending on the perceived value of the project, your ability to manage it, the pay guaranteed and the project scope. Even more importantly, you choose projects depending on whether they fit into your chosen niche or not.

Being choosy doesn't mean pouting off low paying gigs. Low paying gigs might come with a higher perceived value than higher paying ones. They could also challenge your inner designer more.

> **Being choosy means letting a seemingly 'wonderful' project go in case it doesn't fit your ideal or your expertise.**

One of my clients recently sent me feedback about how this was working out for him (I'd suggested he try it out earlier in order to boost his business). I'll call him Andrew*.

Andrew told me that while letting projects pass him by had been difficult, the sacrifice had ultimately started to pay off. He was getting much, much better gigs, he said, and clients only looked for him when such gigs came up.

When I asked him what he based on to accept a gig, he took a moment to think. He later pointed out the project's scope, pay and challenge as the main factors. The main take from all this was that he was no longer running around, looking for clients to hire.

By being choosy, he had established his corner shop, and clients now knew where to find him.

As you might have noticed, being choosy works even better if you, like Andrew, have the ability and skill to pull of projects other designers are more likely to consider difficult or unconventional.

*not the real name

3. Proving Authority on Your Craft

There's a reason people flock to experts and geniuses for all their questions. It's a simple one too: they don't expect a wrong answer. Even in the interior design industry, being an authority sets you apart. It gets you the attention you need to attract better paying clients.

But how do you become an authority in the first place?

By skilling up and learning as much as you can. Being an authority means you understand the most intrinsic details about something, and you know how it works inside out. Working in the industry gives you the experience you need, reading and learning expose you to new ways of doing things.

Once you're better acquainted with your craft, the next step is to make your authority public.

The ways to achieve that are simple. You can speak at community and industry events. You can have an opinion on issues regarding the industry and make it known.

You can offer non-clients on other aspects of interior design. Anything you can do to express your knowledge on the industry without coming off as rude or as a wiseacre.

4. Maintaining Professionalism

People have different ideas of what's deemed professional. For some, it's keeping a safe distance between them and their clients. For others, it's keeping clients close and in the loop. Whatever your idea of professional, maintaining it is one way of positioning yourself.

5. Delivering Quality Work

Positioning is for designers capable of delivering high quality work every time. Clients won't be looking out for you if your work isn't as good as you promise. And as you might already know, quality work always speaks for itself.

In positioning yourself as an expert, you need to start giving clients more than what they expected. You need to surprise them. You need to leave them in awe of your work. And how do you get to that? **By giving your projects your all. By taking chances.**

> **The best designers listen closely to what their clients need, understand what their clients might be thinking and do enough research to offer a difference.**

At the end of the day, it's the quality of work that makes you STAND OUT.

6. Building Relationships

There are two major relationships you have to work on as an interior designer. Your relationships with your clients, and your relationships with other designers.

> **The power of association cannot be understated in the quest to grow your business.**

Every client you get is an opportunity for future client-designer partnerships, and fellow designers have the power to boost your business when you least expect them.

The smallest act of selflessness, such as recommending a friend to a client rather than taking the job, show that you are willing to let others have a go. Directing clients to particular clients is another way. You can also offer clients additional advice beyond the project you're collaborating on.

Sometimes, just supporting a fellow designer by sharing your tools and resources is a good start. Favors don't always result in favor returns though, so don't give them with that in mind. The idea is to build connections that last.

✶ CHAPTER TAKEAWAYS ✶

- ✓ You need a brand of your own - what people think when they see your design business.

- ✓ Every aspect of your brand matters, right from your colour palette to your culture. Make branding decisions that won't damage your business in the long run.

- ✓ You need to *'identity position'* your business right from the start so that you can stand out. To clients, you're just like any other designer. Identity positioning is how to stand apart.

- ✓ It's okay to be choosy about work. If a project is not in your niche, let it go.

- ✓ Relationships are a huge deal in the interior design industry as with any other industry. Build them everyday and you will be grateful.

- ✓ Charge separately for the consultation time, and also for your work. Your consultation time is just as valuable.

CHAPTER 3:

Competitive Analysis

In the world of business, we can't rule out competition. Even monopolies get competitors over time as suppliers learn the secrets of the trade.

In a fair, normally functioning economy, there will always be someone else offering a similar product or service; in this case, interior design and architectural services.

Some regions and cities are more conducive for designers, with only a handful of designers legally registered there. Others, not so much. Designers in metropolitan areas in developed countries find themselves with way more competition as more and more designers move there and set up shop.

If this is your current situation, neither identity positioning nor having the best services is sufficient enough a feature in getting you the attention you need from potential clients. Hundreds of other savvy designers will be doing the same.

As a designer trying to grow your business, you can't afford to stay at the bottom of the pack with everyone else. You need to beat the competition out of the game. Not literally of course, but by outwitting them. That's where competitive analysis comes in.

Competitive analysis involves you getting a deeper understanding of your competitors, i.e. the other interior design service providers in your current area. It involves getting to know the details of how they operate, how they draw in – and keep - clients, how they structure their services and other important details.

The idea is to understand how they've positioned their services in the market so that you can get an idea of how to position yours in a unique, better way that will draw clients.

Now I know from years of experience that many interior designers find this tasking and unnecessary. Some think competitive analysis and other related 'gimmicks' should be left to big, product based multinational companies like Coca Cola whose products face daily battle with other similar products in the murky world of fickle consumer tastes.

Other industry professionals I've spoken to believe competitive analysis to be intrusive and unethical to a larger extent. But I disagree. To put it simply, all these points of view are wrong and uninformed.

Competitive analysis is necessary for any kind of business in any industry as long as it has viable competitors. And no, it isn't intrusive in any way unless those using it employ illegal and unrealistic methods of gaining private information about competitors.

I personally see competitive analysis as a power boost, just like the kind you see in video games, or that magical spot on the *Snakes and Ladders* game board that propels you ahead.

When done right, as many interior designers already do today, competitive analysis will take you from Square 1 to Square 10 in half the time others take to get to Square 5! You get to skip the ever so disappointing try-and-fail loop.

***

The Benefits of Using Competitive Analysis

One of my earliest clients, a middle aged Indian mother of three I'll call Mehal shuddered the most when I told her about competitive analysis. It was 2016, and she had been running her business for almost a year in Mumbai.

Following a series of government investment deals with foreign companies, the city was now leaping into a new kind of metropolis as new multinational companies set up offices and commissioned new buildings.

Her area of preference, office interior design, was picking up. But unlike many of her peers, business wasn't catching up. When she contacted me that October afternoon, I immediately recognized how unique her issue was.

It's not that Mehal wasn't established yet; she was. She'd been in the industry long enough and had a number of completed gigs under her belt. But Mehal felt like the soil was shifting under her feet.

She felt like there were too many people now competing for the new lucrative jobs, and she was suffocating under the strain. What seemed like a season of endless opportunity was turning into a major disappointment. All the old methods of getting clients were not working any more either.

That's when I suggested that she look deeply at her competitors to see what they were doing and how they were doing it.

Initially, she balked at the idea of competitive analysis as a solution to these problems. It would only cost more time and money, she complained, yet what she felt she needed was a quick, workable solution.

Later on, a few more hours of pestering and coercion finally did the trick. Mehal decided she would study her competitors' every move but only as long as she used legal methods. I gave her a go-ahead.

What she discovered about them weeks later blew her mind, and opened it up at the same time (more on that later). The bottom line is that Mehal learned a lot more than she'd expected, and not just about what other designers were doing, but what she wasn't doing right.

Much like with Mehal, competitive analysis will accord you a series of benefits. You will get to know who your targeted audience really are and what they really like, how your competitors are wooing their clients (including their sketchiest tricks), how your competitors are gaining market traction and what they are doing wrong.

You'll then determine how you can uniquely market yourself to potential clients without looking so much like the competition. Most importantly, you'll save yourself a lot more time, and like Mehal, avert avoidable mistakes easily.

***

How to Analyse Your Competitors

Competitive analysis essentially involves trying to know everything about how your competitors operate, both externally and internally. That requires information from a wide range of sources, especially since some businesses are notoriously secretive.

To get started, I suggest you consider at the following resources.
- Internet articles and archives
- Trade journals
- Quarterly and annual reports
- Trade releases
- Press statements
- Press mentions and interviews
- Former clients of your competitors
- Fellow designers
- Becoming a customer

***

What to Look for?

While carrying out competitive analysis, look out for information on the following:

1. Your Competitors

Who are your direct competitors? You should define your competitor as anyone offering the same services as you do, or anyone that bears similarity to what you do or the clients you work for.

As an interior designer, your competition are your fellow designers, both established and upcoming. Look out for them. Note their past gigs. Note their former clients. Note their business addresses.

2. Your Competitors' Service Range

Following the list of competitors, you've drawn, identify the services each offers. What niche are they experts in? What Projects have they completed?

3. Your Competitors' Strengths and Weaknesses

This is the most important aspect of the whole process. The analysis you carry out here helps you dissect each competitor so you can delve into their underbelly and see them beyond the marquee.

An interior design business's strength can be anything from top talent to a strong, distinctive portfolio. It can also be its book of contacts. Discover the strengths each of your competitors rely on.

In the same spirit, delve in for the weaknesses. No business, not even the best financed or most popular ones, runs sans a couple of weaknesses. And they are not always visible; smart designers do a good job of hiding their cracks.

Dolly's Interior Design Studio next door may have the top talent but still struggle with a terrible reputation of a history of incomplete projects and costliness. Only former clients and gossip columnists may know that. But that's the catch you need.

Here's why: Solving a need – that's the major reason new businesses and ideas continue trumping big, existing companies today despite the latter's market share and strong financial footing.

If the new business solves a problem that the older business couldn't solve in its lifetime, customers are left with no choice but to shift allegiance. Finding out what the old business has failed to solve and creating the solution instead is one good example of exploiting a company's weaknesses.

4. Your Competitors' Existing Strategies for Achieving Goals

Strategies in this sense are basically the approaches your competitors have in place for achieving their goals. The question to ask here, essentially, is 'How is designer X working toward achieving goal ABC?'.

Businesses must have a marketing strategy, an advertising strategy, a customer acquisition and retention strategy and so on. Finding information on some of these strategies, such as an advertising strategy only requires basic watching of how a company rolls out ads across various mediums.

I also suggest attending industry events and getting personal interviews with former clients or staff from the competitor business. Some strategies however, such as customer acquisition and retention, require deeper observation. I suggest going undercover for such. *Here's how:*

- ❖ **Identify the social media funnels your clients are using.**
  Interior designers have since identified the power of the internet as an advertising, marketing and communication tool with prospective clients and the rest of the world. Many now put it to good use, social media even more so.

  Nowadays, almost every designer has a glowing website, or a YouTube vlog, or an Instagram page filled with lust-worthy photos of past gigs. Some just use Facebook, while others stick with Tumblr or Twitter accounts.

Others go further with videos, podcasts, monthly newsletters, webinars, industry forum postings, the whole lot. Your job here is to identify all the different channels your competitors are using daily.

- **Sign up for their channels**
  The next step is to subscribe to these channels yourself. The idea is that you need to experience first-hand what each designer is doing with their clients through these channels, and what better way is there than subscription?

  Don't worry about email backlog; subscriptions can always be cancelled and inboxes cleaned.

- **Mark their different customer acquisition techniques**
  After signing up, it's time to snoop around. Look around their websites and channel pages? How are they set up? Regarding customer engagement, how are they keeping you in the loop? Newsletters? Free books? Q&A sessions? Nothing?

  If they do send any promotional materials, notice the details, like how they structure their copy and how they keep you coming back. How do they structure their content? Who is it targeted to? What tools are they using? Take some notes.

- **Identify their different partnerships with other service providers**
  Some interior designers work hand in hand with other companies in a bid to build strong client referral programs. A design studio working with a beverages company to offer free couches and carpeting to the first 5 winners of a soda-based game show is an example of a strategic partnership.

  Some partnerships are classic lock-in agreements, such as when an interior designer partners with a restaurant chain to redo all their restaurants across a city. Other partnerships are designed to draw in new clients by offering them exclusive services.

  Identify any partnerships your competitors are part of. Analyze how they operate and what makes them work.

- **Existing trends in the industry**
  I always remind my clients to look at the data and see if they can identify any trends or patterns in how other designers get their gigs or manage their businesses. Patterns give you valuable insight into what is currently working and what isn't.

I've had clients who realized, after doing analysis, that their advertising means of choice, the business card, had long gone out of fashion in their city. Other designers had long picked up with alternatives like portfolios on websites.

Mehal, my designer client from above, discovered, through a series of meetings over coffee with trusted colleagues and the random journalist, that most of the interior designers scooping up gigs were doing it differently altogether.

Most were going for long term contracts, not the one time gig she was used to. Some were full contracts with building owners, commissioning them to design whole floors and stuff like that.

Others were more specific, like contracts to design a series of elegant homes in a Mumbai suburb that were being built for foreign expats. What struck her most was how these designers were marketing themselves.

According to inside sources she spoke to, the old portfolio was no longer the required device to get a foot in the door. Designers were meeting building commissioners at city parties, at event openings and through referrals. Portfolios had started to come in last, as a formal gesture of professionalism.

The referrals also drew her attention to the slew of partnerships that had developed, especially among architects and particular design studios. As it happened, each was recommending the other, with the top brass turning down contracts if their recommendations weren't accepted.

At the end of the day, Mehal realized that she was doing it all wrong. Some of the techniques she'd previously relied on were now way out of tune with the new changes. If she wanted a part of the cake, she knew she was going to have to make quick, major shifts to her approach.

***

How to Use the Data You Get

The information you collect from your competitive analysis excursion is of no use if you don't put it to work.

Remember that the reason behind collecting this information is for you to understand how other designers are making it work so that you too can derive a strategy of your own. This strategy is supposed to utilize the gaps and weaknesses they display.

- Identify common trends from the data, such as whether all other designers are using a particular marketing tactic instead of another. Also note whether trends have changed over a period of time. Try to work out why.

- Identify differences between you and other designers. What software are they using? How different are their client acquisition tactics from yours? What are they doing different that you're not?

- Identify the strategies that are working for other designers and explore them down to the smallest detail to understand how they work. Is it a particular customer retention tactic? How do they employ it? See how you can incorporate them into your design business.

- Discover what doesn't work. Even successful designers have failures. See what didn't work for them and why. It could be a new logo, a new niche, anything.

- Identify your unique strength. This can be something all other designers are spending a lot to acquire, such as machinery or new clients, or something they can't have, such as your skillset. See how you can use that to leverage unsure clients.

- Chart the future of your industry. Where is it going? What trends do you see? How can you position your business to take advantage of future industry shifts?

✱ CHAPTER TAKEAWAYS ✱

✓ Competitive analysis is not a bad thing. It's not illegal either, unless you incorporate illegal methods into your process.

✓ You shouldn't do competitive analysis just to blatantly copy other designers. Rather, learn from their mistakes.

✓ There's always something to learn from your competitors. If you can, learn how you can solve a problem they do not solve.

✓ Competitive analysis also involves honest dissection of your business to see your weaknesses, strengths, opportunities and threats, and how they stack with those of other designers. Don't forget to judge your business.

✓ Data from your analysis is no use if you don't use it to improve your business.

CHAPTER 4:

Narrowing Down Your Niche

In this section we look at why you need to further narrow down your niche, right after setting up your brand.

I know we earlier talked about choosing a niche in the market for you to specialize in, as part of finding your place in the industry. This section follows that idea by expanding the notion a little.

> **You may revisit "Chapter 1: Finding Your Place in The Interior Design Industry" to remind yourself of basics on "Why you should choose a niche", "How to Determine your niche".**

Here we'll go straight down to narrowing down your niche further.

***

Narrowing Your Niche

The interior design industry, as you may already know, is comprised of different sections, all requiring different skill specifications and having different clients who need them. These sections are what we call niches.

People usually categorize niches under a few distinct categories including Real Estate, Residential, Commercial, and Hospitality. But niches can be molded out of other factors such as income of clients, geographical location, scope of gig etc.

Some designers crossover into every niche; restaurants, lighting, window design, furniture, hotels, home remodels etc. But that is not the route I recommend. As a designer looking to grow your design business twofold, you need to niche down.

That means settling for one niche, say, restaurants, as I earlier mentioned in Section 2. The clients from the restaurant niche become your target market. But finding your target market is not enough to set your business on the path to steady growth.

That's why you need to narrow down your niche further.

> **Narrowing down your niche involves breaking down your chosen niche further to select those clients that are directly in need of your services and are more likely to order for them.**

I call these ideal/target clients; I refer to their sections within your niche as sub niches.

Take the example of the restaurant niche. There are many types of restaurants – the average city can have everything from Michelin-starred restaurants to low key 10 table hideouts.

All of them become potential clients when you choose the niche. But you need to specialize even further. The sub niches here are various; you can stick to smaller, artsy restaurants or go for diners.

You can also go for hotel restaurants instead. Or you can stick with a particular aspect of the design for these restaurants, such as lighting or furniture only. The idea is to specialize so well in something that you become the go-to for it.

Narrowing down gets you the same benefits as choosing a niche, only they are more this time. The most important reason is that it gets you more credibility as a designer, which can only be a good thing.

The other fact is that you get to compete with less people for clients. So many other designers are grasping around for every gig they can get. You, on the other hand, get to blur out everyone else and focus your attention on clients that actually need your service.

That's why, because the clients in your sub niche are more likely to order for your services, narrowing down actually improves your chances of nailing your first clients (if you're just starting out).

When narrowing down to a specific sub niche, ask yourself these questions:
1. What are all the possible sub niches available under my chosen niche?
2. What sub niche am I most comfortable with among them all?
3. Which sub niche is the least subscribed to by designers?

4. What sub niche aligns best with my skills and capabilities?
5. Which sub niche is more profitable?
6. What do I have to do to make a mark in each of the sub niches?

Find a list of interior design sub niches you can go for here (www.searchmetry.com/interior-design-marketing/interior-designing-specializations).

✶ CHAPTER TAKEAWAYS ✶

✓ Niches can be quite wide. Even within a niche, you need to get specific.

✓ Running after all forms of clients isn't always the best practice.

✓ Don't be confused - narrowing down within in a niche comes with tons of benefits for your business.

CHAPTER 5:

Identifying Your Target Clients

In this section we'll cover the concept of the ideal client, plus the basics on why you need to know your exact client and how you can identify them beforehand.

Now that you've settled into a niche of your choice and identified the sub-niches that you are most comfortable with, the next step is to conquer the 'client'. Here's a simple fact: anyone can be your client.

Anyone, anywhere on the globe, can want your services and ask for them. But that's the last thing you want to bet on if you want to grow your interior design business. You need proper clients, the kind that 'need' your services and understand what you do.

Now, understandably, you must be expecting your clients to come from within your chosen niche and that's okay. But that's the slower route to growing your business the way you want. Every other designer is doing that.

As I mentioned in an earlier chapter, you need to be unique. That's why you need target clients. Target clients are more specific, and twice as likely to order for your services because they actually 'need' them. In other words, they are your ideal clients.

I first got introduced to the idea of knowing your target clients from the very beginning by **Paul Anderson**, an old friend and interior designer based in New York. He had set up a stall at a home interiors and design fair organised by a major paint company.

We were chatting on Skype about his experience there when he revealed to me his astonishing approach to netting paying customers.

Paul had set up a stall like everyone else; his was along one of the temporary walls marking the edge of the fair space. He described to me in great detail how he interacted with visitors to his stall throughout the day.

I still remember he said that first visitor was an older, stocky man with glasses, who came to admire the model houses on display. He revealed that his wife was in the process of redesigning the new family home he'd bought but he wasn't sure she was getting it right.

After a few more minutes of conversation littered with admiration for the house models, the man moved on to the next stall. The fair became twice as busy after the lunch break. During that time, more than 50 people dropped by his stall, some of them couples.

One piece of detail stood out for me. Paul said that he was giving out his business card and a brochure, but not to every stall visitor. And he wasn't just hoarding them either; he said he had two full boxes of both with him.

When I asked him why, Paul told me that he was giving his card to his ideal clients only, not everyone. He believed that giving out one's card and portfolio was a good strategy, but only with the right potential clients. His point struck a chord with me.

Later I had to ask how he identified his ideal client. Paul took care to explain that his target/ideal client was the young married couple in a new home, possibly with kids or a pet. Almost immediately my risk alarm went off.

Such an unapologetic narrow-down of the client base felt risky to me, and more so in our industry, but he didn't seem fearful. Instead he pointed at his brochure, and told me he'd structured it to meet his ideal clients' tastes and preferences.

Giving the brochure out to anyone would have been a waste of resources, he added, because the services wouldn't have appealed to them anyway. I was nearly sold by then, but then I realized he still had half his brochures at the end of the day.

Was it better to intentionally lose 80% of your stall visitors in favour of 20% that you thought were the right kind of client? Yes, he told me. He wasn't worried at all. Rather than have his business card and brochures taken by everyone and then trashed the moment they left the fair, he believed it was smarter to save each brochure for clients that actually had need for them. *His target clients.*

In fact, he believed that the 80% loss in clients had been an avoidable oversight, so he was planning to switch stalls in favour of a location next to a series of stalls selling household goods, which he knew his target clients would frequent.

A few weeks later we Skyped again. The fair had ended well enough and it was back to business. This time, Paul didn't wait for me to ask about the results of his strategy.

He told me that in the weeks following the fair, he'd received more than 35 calls about his services, 15 of which had culminated into dates for future appointments with him about his services. He was content with the result.

With a different plan, Paul Anderson would probably have received 20 calls overall despite having given out all his brochures. And only about a quarter of those would have extended into future appointments. **The reason**: he'd have spent time and money on the wrong clients.

That was about 4 years ago. Ever since then, I've met interior designers whose target customer base surprised me. Earlier in my career I'd have thought they were crazy to be so specific. Now I knew they were doing it better than anyone else.

Gay couples living in apartments regardless of age. High ranking women with a taste for class. Conservative middle-aged couples living in the suburbs. Middle aged women running large Indian family homes. You get the picture.

The variety was striking, but so was the specificity. If you notice, both gay couples and middle-aged matriarchs running large households are good potential clients for any interior designer in the home design niche, but they aren't specific enough for one designer. Each had to be taken up by someone else that understood their needs better.

The idea is that not all clients who come knocking at your door will be your ideal clients.

I have since picked up this ideal client mantra and expanded it for my clients, who I believe it has helped greatly. Ultimately, and through a live example, Paul Anderson made me realise the difference between potential clients and target clients.

Target clients are different from potential clients. Potential clients are everywhere. They may be interested in your sub niche or not. But they can still hire you, because they have need for design services that fall within your general niche at the end of the day.

Target customers, on the other hand, need your services. Whatever you offer is what they need. They fit inside your sub niche like a baby in a womb. You know that because you understand their lives, their characteristics, their jobs, their future plans and most importantly, their tastes.

Target Market Vs Target Audience

The above variation between potential and ideal clients always stirs some confusion over the difference between a target market and a target audience.

A **target market** is the overall group of people that you try to sell your services to. In the case of an interior designer, that would be the clients interested in your niche. Potential clients come from target markets.

A **target audience**, on the other hand, is a specific group of people within the target market that you direct specific services at courtesy of their unique needs. A target market can have more than one target audience, based on different quirks and preferences. Target clients come from target audiences.

The benefits of identifying your target clients

When consulting with my clients, I always call it the three-step assurance strategy: *identity positioning, choosing a niche* and *identifying target clients*. When combined, all three give you a soundproof start to growing your interior design business minus the mistakes. Identifying your target clients ranks highest among the three.

The very first clients I asked to identify their target clients had the exact reaction I expected. They laughed it off, calling it largely unnecessary and unrealistic. Most of them believed it would ultimately undermine their overall goal of doubling growth, which they were convinced was to be achieved by accumulating more clients on their rosters.

I wasn't surprised; I'd thought the same the first time I heard of it. But Paul Anderson's real-life example came in handy here, especially when I was dealing with the first clients to try it out.

When one of my Bangladesh-based clients called back over Skype a month later to relay how the strategy had netted her two new clients in the space of a week, I felt a sudden rush of joy. I guess it came from knowing me and my clients had found another way to make growth possible without spending a fortune.

I've identified a series of benefits you'll accrue from identifying your target clients from the beginning. Almost all my clients have experienced one or all of them since fully employing the technique.

❖ **You'll cut costs with better financial planning**. That's because you won't spend money on advertising and marketing to everyone but to only those that actually need your service. That's usually a smaller cluster of individuals or companies and they don't always need to be remarketed to over and over again.

- **You'll get to plan and structure your message properly before pitching to clients**, so you can get their attention with less mistakes. The message in this case is what you're offering and how it fits into their lives and solves their problem. Creating this message becomes way easier when looking at target clients.

- **You'll save boatloads of time because target clients have specific needs,** and you understand them. No hours spent explaining to a client why they might need new living room furnishing in the first place.

- **You'll design effective sales and marketing campaigns that actually convert.** Conversion is when your marketing message reaches out to a client and entices them to check out your portfolio or even hire you. Sales and marketing campaigns are always prone to quick failure because of all the uncertainty, but knowing your target client changes that.

- **You'll get trusty direction** on the content you ought to generate for your business and online presence, be it YouTube self-help videos or web articles or podcasts, depending on your clients' needs, their station in life and other factors.

- **You'll easily identify ideas for new products**, services and service associations that your target clients might need now or in the future, basing on their existing needs.

- **You'll get free guidance** on how to structure offers and deals that clients can't look away from.

- **You'll learn how to segment your email and social media campaigns** judging by each target market and what converts best with them.

- **You'll get better at managing client expectations beforehand** because then you know who they are and what they are looking for. That means turning down clients with expectations that surpass what you can offer, and vice versa.

The best part about identifying target clients is that it doesn't force your other clients to stop working with you. It just helps you focus your services on people that understand your message better.

But before you can start reaping any benefits from target clients, you must have them in place. Remember that target clients are not every client in your niche, but a select group with needs that align best with your design services.

How to identify your target clients.

> To be able to attract your dream clients to your interior design business, you should have a clear picture of your dream client in mind. The question here is, who are you looking for? Because if you don't know who you are looking for, how will you know when you find them?

I know there's a ton of ideas I can suggest to use for identifying clients, but not all are appropriate for interior designers. The few I recommend include, in summary:

- **Identify the specific problem you can solve/you're already solving** – then ask yourself: which segment of your target market has these problems?

- **Look at your competitors** – what are they serving the clients you share? What aren't they serving well? Then look for how to position yourself to offer it better.

- **Use analytical data**, especially that provided by Google Analytics about who's visited your website or portfolio and done what. This is particularly good for identifying target clients by geographical location.

- **Conduct surveys and interviews** within your target market to see what potential clients actually think about your service, and whether they really find it useful. Surveys can be formal (research-like interviews or over the phone) or informal (through conversations in the park or over coffee, maybe).

- **Look at what you're offering,** and then determine the segment in your target market needs it most or would find it super useful.

- **Look at your current clients:** who have you worked for recently? That's who your ad message reached out to the first time. Their characteristics are a good starting point when choosing other target clients. Also, who among your existing clients would you like to work for again?

- **Create a buyer persona for your ideal client.** Buyer personas have long been a staple in marketing campaigns. They are a virtual representation of the ideal customer before you get to meet them or introduce your product. Creating a buyer persona is a whole process on its own.

1. **Create an avatar for the ideal client.**

An avatar is like a summarized ID of your presumed target client. It covers everything from their physical description to what they need and how they need it.

First, you need to define the target client. You can also have more than one target client if you're trying to compare between two or more specific sub-niches.

Here's an illustration of client definition, assuming the residential design and furnishing niche.

> **Jack Barr**, represents single male bachelor niche
> High level ranking executive at work that's interested in trendy, tasteful home furnishing from time to time.
>
> Or
>
> **Anna Smith and John Smith**, representing 'married couple living in the 'burbs' niche
>
> Full time parents with a growing family, interested in affordable and practical home furnishing and renovations from time to time
>
> Or
>
> **John and Jack**, representing 'young gay couple' niche
> Self-aware individuals looking for classy, slightly over the top designs on a regular basis in time with existing trends.

These aren't the only types of personas you can create. Remember that personas are developed by you, depending on what you think the ideal client for your services will be.

To make developing your ideal client's buyer persona easier, I've published an article here (www.searchmetry.com/interior-design-marketing/ideal-clients-buyer-persona). I recommend it for fleshing out your target clients the way you envision them in only a few minutes.

---

2. **Outline the buyer persona**

The next step is to outline the buyer persona using their supposed characteristics. The good people over at **Digital Marketer** (www.digitalmarketer.com) had very good information regarding the creation of a persona. Some of it is shared below.

I've added an illustration to each persona example to draw a picture of how it ought to be done. The illustration uses four attributes: **demographic information, goals and values, sources of information** and **challenges/pain points**.

Demographic information

Demo data is the basis of everything. There are no target clients – or clients to market to at all – if there is no demographic data about them. This data gives life to your buyer persona so it has to be specific.

Illustration of sample demographic information
Age: 41
Gender: Male
Marital status: Single
Children: No
Their age: NIL
Home location: Hyderabad/Mumbai
Level of education: Postgraduate
Employed: Yes
Occupation: Banker
Job title: C-suite level
Average monthly income: 40, 000 INR
Quote/Mantra/Life philosophy: Each mistake is a learning point.
Others: Loves hanging out at alternative clubs

Goals and Values

The goals and values of your target client directly connect you to their needs and underlying driving forces.

Values highlight what your ideal clients believe in, and what they are committed to. Goals are what they intend to achieve within a given period of time.

Illustration: Goals
Suggestions:
⇒ **Jack Barr**: to get a one-time design job that's practical, trendy and incorporates his style.
⇒ **Anna and John Smith**: to have a beautiful house interior within a month without all the planning and hard work

⇒ **John and Jack**: to have their apartments similar to a dope photo they saw on Pinterest and apartmenttherapy.com

Illustration: Values
  Suggestions: is committed to -
    ⇒ **Jack Barr**: Minimalism
    ⇒ **Anna and John Smith**: Using eco-friendly products
    ⇒ **John and Jack**: Cultural appropriation

Their Sources of Information
   A person's sources of information are a direct window into what they are interested in, what their life revolves around and what their mindset is.

Readers of *Architectural Digest*, for example, aren't always expected to have the same level of understanding of interior design and its intricacies with readers of, say, *Sports Illustrated*.

Both are highly popular magazines aimed at different groups of people. Highlighting your target clients' sources of information can also help you identify the websites you can advertise on for better conversion in future campaigns.

While mapping out sources of information, go for sources that you think only that client would use and no one else would. That is important for singling the target client out.

Illustration

John Barr

  ⇒ **Books**: The Habits of Highly Effective People, Minimalism: Live a Meaningful Life, The One Minute Manager
  ⇒ **Newspapers/Magazines**: Architectural Digest, Wired, Men's Health, The New Yorker, The Wall Street Journal
  ⇒ **Blogs/Websites**: dariusforoux.com, The Art of Manliness, Man Made DIY
  ⇒ **TV Shows**: The Apprentice, The Rachel Maddow Show

Anna and John Smith

  ⇒ **Books**: The Life Changing Magic of Tidying Up, Organized Simplicity, Clutter free with Kids
  ⇒ **Newspapers/Magazines**: Good Housekeeping, People, Real Simple

⇒ **Blogs/Websites**: BBC Good Food, Marriage 365, Unveiled Wife
⇒ **TV Shows**: Fixer Upper, CNN News, Judge Judy

<u>Jack and John</u>
⇒ **Newspapers/Magazines**: Out, Attitude, Entertainment Weekly
⇒ **Blogs/Websites**: Bitches Gotta Eat, The Art of Manliness, Man Made DIY
⇒ **TV Shows**: RuPaul's Drag Race, 2 Travel Dads, Gay Parenting Voices

Challenges and Pain Points

Knowing the possible challenges and pain points your target client could currently have in getting a service like yours is a direct way to identify their changing needs. Plus, you get a window into new products and services they might need in future.

Challenges
He/she could be challenged with:
⇒ A smaller budget than necessary
⇒ Finding a designer that understands their unique needs

Pain points
He/she could have pain points like:
⇒ Lack of an exact idea of what they want
⇒ Lack of enough free time on their hands

From the personas above, you can identify the stark differences that define each individual. Those differences directly influence how you market your design business to each one of them.

Ideally, you only need to start with one buyer persona, say, like John Barr. You can always create other personas when you decide to branch out to other sub niches within your niche.

✼ CHAPTER TAKEAWAYS ✼

✓ Target market and target audience are two different audiences.

✓ You need a target audience for your interior design business. Those are the people that really need your service.

- ✓ Marketing is no use if you are marketing to the wrong crowd. Don't waste your marketing materials and dollars on the wrong audience.
- ✓ To know your target audience, you'll need to put some effort into understanding who they are and what they need.
- ✓ Create buyer personas for the people you think are your ideal audience. It makes understanding your target audience easier.

CHAPTER 6:

Setting Up Your Marketing Plan

In this section, we look at the marketing aspect of your interior design business.

After you've identified your target client and understood who they really are, the next step is to market your services to them. Because you have an idea of who they are and what they need, marketing to them won't be like a blind run into a sandstorm the same way marketing to a whole potential market is.

Still, I press that marketing for interior designers is different. The techniques used may be the same as with other businesses, but the approaches tend to differ.

For a business like yours that's trying to stand out and grow twofold in a saturated market, conventional marketing techniques are not the way to go. They're good, but not for your kind and size of business.

I've always found it more rewarding to diversify your marketing and promotion techniques and do some intense targeting so as to spend less and gain more.

Below I have identified a collection of techniques, platforms and strategies that work. Most have already been employed by my clients and given favourable reviews.

Establishing Expert Persona

In an earlier section, we discussed the power of being an expert or appearing like one, in front of your target market.

The power of an expert persona cannot be underestimated; it's the reason Tim Ferris shuts down whole rooms when he talks and other podcasters don't. It's the reason *Architectural Digest* magazine is subscribed to by millions and hundreds of other interior design magazines aren't.

It's also the reason other interior designers are bagging gig after gig and you're not.

They're either experts at what they do, or they've positioned themselves to look like it. Here's the fun fact: it always pays to be or appear to be an expert.

The Oxford English Dictionary defines an expert as *a person who is very knowledgeable about or skilful in a particular area*. Other definitions picture an expert as *a specialist or authority on a particular subject, someone with all the answers*.

Who doesn't want a specialist to solve their problems? Mostly those who are constrained, financially or otherwise. The point is, people trust a specialist to be able to solve whatever problem they're facing. And so the demand for a specialist is very high. In other words, an expert persona will get you more clients than an ordinary-designer persona.

There are a series of steps I've directed my clients to go when creating their personas. Each of them has had varying results but all have always performed as expected.

- **Get knowledgeable**. Research on different topics and see how they connect with your area of interest, i.e. interior design. You don't want to be the expert that can't see simple correlations between interior design and other industries.

- **Get your opinions published on major platforms**. That could be microblogging platforms like Medium, or major websites like HuffPost, or in opinion columns on interior design platforms like Houzz. This helps people identify you as a credible source to rely on.

- **Answer questions on forums and answer websites**. The more credible a forum is, the better. Even better, the more answers you give, the more views your answers get.

- **Quora's 'Interior design' and 'Home furnishing' sections are a good start** if you're into home furnishing. Other forums, like those managed by interior design websites and platforms, are also a good choice.

- **Create your own platform online for hosting your opinions**. If you can't easily find spots on other platforms, you can always create your own. Websites, podcasts, forums, the whole bit.

- **Speak at industry events and local design gatherings**. Getting a chance to speak at an event hosted by colleagues in the same industry is pure gold. Just make sure you have sensible information to pass over. Make your speeches resourceful and memorable and you'll be on your way to expert status.

NB: They don't have to be large industry gatherings. Even small, local housing or design related events are a starting point. Art and museum events, town hall debates on housing, local designer conferences and meetups, anywhere where your voice will be heard.

- **Create solutions, not complaints**. Others may be content blaming something. Not you. You should only offer solutions that are proven to work.

- **Build your portfolio**. Appearing as an expert only lasts long enough. People will want to look at the design work you've done, and you had better have something to show them. You build your portfolio by tackling major projects and doing your best.

Creating A Marketing Funnel

I never thought of marketing funnels as a worthy strategy to teach my clients until I used it for my own firm and saw its wonderful, actionable results.

Nowadays, judging from my experience with them, I believe marketing funnels are some of the better ideas to come out of the marketing conferences I attended in the last 10 years.

Designers have always found it a confusing term. But it's quite the opposite. Think of an actual funnel and its torch shaped design - bigger at the top, like a wide bowl opening, and way smaller at the bottom.

In marketing, a marketing funnel is a way of identifying how customers are engaging with your marketing campaign and your products. It is usually divided into five regions; Interest, Engagement, Evaluation, Commitment and Purchase.

At the very top of the funnel, your marketing strategy appeals to everyone that's interested. That's why it's wide – everyone steps in. As the customers go further down the funnel, some drop out, hence the funnel's smaller width.

By the time you get to the end of the funnel (Purchase stage), very few customers have stayed put, hence the very small opening.

Marketing funnels work for interior design businesses too, and for both online and offline offerings. They work everywhere, whether it's getting people to sign up for a newsletter, buy a product or divulge their contacts.

The number of customers that are retained/lost along the way, starting from when they click on a display ad to when they actually sign up for something or request a demo or offer their custom is seen with a marketing funnel.

The biggest advantage of a funnel is that it helps you identify how your campaign is working. You can easily identify where you're losing customers and what you can do to fix it.

Assuming you've created a funnel and you realize half of your leads (the people that clicked on your ad somewhere on the web or picked up a brochure you placed somewhere etc.) are dropping out just after divulging their contacts or seeing the homepage, you can devise a strategy to keep future leads in the loop until they see your portfolio or actually visit your offices.

That's something only a marketing funnel can show you. So how can interior designers take advantage of this strategy? I have a few proven tricks I've used myself.

First, you identify your goal. What do you need? Brand awareness? New clients? Awareness of a new service? Signups to your website? Shares across the web for your portfolio? New orders? New contacts for your email list? New eyeballs on your portfolio? Anything can be a goal.

Just make sure it's measurable for future retargeting purposes. The next step is to figure out how to get your leads to make that goal happen.

How will you get people to make it happen? By drawing a roadmap of what they'll do and offering breadcrumbs to guide them along the way. Where will people go after clicking on your website ad? Is your homepage a good landing spot? Experts say no.

Isn't it better to land on a page that explains the advert in details? Maybe. Where do they go after? A 'sign up' page? Not a good idea. How about they go to a 'Buy' or 'Add to cart' page first? Better.

This is the kind of roadmap you need to draw out. Most importantly, you have to figure out the possible roadblocks at each stage of the purchase process and weed them out.

Create a cookie for people to bite. This is what draws people initially to your funnel in the first place.

It can be a compelling advert on a website or in the subway, a social media advert, a draw or discount event, a free e-book (with your contacts inside of course), anything to turn people's head.

Set up your landing page (or landing ground if you're going offline instead). So where do people go once they've entered your funnel? If it's an online cookie, you need a landing page. That's where all your links will redirect to and where your visitors will find the next stage of the process.

The latter can be anything from sign up forms to a demo of your products and services to statistics about your design firm to a 'Buy' page for your services. It should be able to lead them to your next stage, whether it's purchasing a service or booking one, just viewing your portfolio.

For offline cookies, you can still use an online landing page by displaying links to your website or social media pages on print materials. You can also display your phone contacts and address for future visits. Even call-to actions work here, like '*See More in store Today*' or '*Get a Quote Before Today Ends*'.

Be ready to make quick changes. Monitoring the metrics of your campaign is important for gauging its success. It's these metrics that help you see where more people are dropping out and why.

Assuming you discover that people are getting to your website alright, browsing your portfolio and ...wait for it.... leaving for another website instead of calling the phone number you've displayed at the top of the page as expected, do you just sit back and worry? You do the opposite.

You find a way for them to see the phone number more often until they are triggered to call you about what they've seen. Such is the required flexibility that keeps campaigns flourishing.

Retargeting Funnels

As a follow-up to a marketing funnel, an even more interesting concept takes shape: a retargeting funnel. Just like the retargeting we know, the retargeting funnel looks to draw back the potential clients you lost along the way to the bottom of the funnel by using new techniques.

Retargeting is already a highly recommended technique for reigniting interest; the retargeting funnel essentially follows that same strategy by creating a retargeting tactic at each level of the funnel.

The funnel banks on the leads you've already got and targets them with differently worded emails, new adverts targeted at the websites they visit, etc.

I strongly recommend that at each stage of the funnel/customer acquisition, you create a different tactic for retargeting the many potential clients who have not moved to the next stage the first time around.

Don't let potential clients pass you by. Your first actual well-paying gig could come from someone that's marketed to thrice before they agree to check out your portfolio.

Guerrilla Marketing

The telecom giant Vodafone once did the unthinkable in Romania. It hired professional pickpockets and had them stuff promotional flyers from Vodafone into people's bags, pockets, coats, purses, everywhere.

If at this point, you're wondering what the management at Vodafone Romania was thinking, you're not alone. But there was a reason for the whole spectacle.

Up until then, the company had seen only meagre results from their efforts to promote their Vodafone phone insurance program and its benefits.

The statistics were even less forgiving – at the time, a phone was being stolen in Romania every 2 minutes. Still, people weren't paying the expected attention.

The company had gone the traditional route of advertising in its first attempts to alert the public to their insurance program, all in vain. That's when the pickpocketing campaign was decided upon.

As results show, people reported surprise and shock at finding flyers in their pockets and purses on getting home, flyers they hadn't picked up anywhere. It also opened their eyes to how vulnerable they were to thieves and pickpockets even in seemingly safe places.

Vodafone's aim had been to make people see this vulnerability and turn to its phone insurance program. It's safe to conclude now that their crazy and unusual marketing attempt worked.

More importantly, it worked better and faster than traditional print or TV ads would have. Such is the attention-grabbing and conversion power of guerrilla marketing.

Guerrilla marketing is unique is different from the more traditional forms of marketing. Wikipedia defines it as *an advertisement strategy concept designed for businesses to promote their services in an unconventional way with little budget to spend.* Note the 'unconventional' and 'little budget' here.

One of the promotional materials for the epic 2012 world destruction movie '2012' was a wall-length poster covering two walls of corridors in major public walkways in some American cities. You couldn't miss its design.

The poster, which actually ran for a stunning length of wall on both sides, seemed to have blue water overflowing from it into the corridor from both sides, but never extending further than a few feet into the corridor.

Because of that design, walking into the corridor felt like walking into an aquarium of sorts without the water. And despite the water not being real, the poster immediately drew you in and stuck to memory long after.

Which, suffice to say, is what the marketing people wanted. And that's just one level of 'unconventional'.

How unconventional does American underwear company GoldToe's move to dress up some of New York's most visible statues in underwear as part of their marketing campaign sound? *Extremely unconventional.*

In other words, your guerrilla tactic can be anything from floating couches on your local Main Street to a free fun platform that allows people to recreate their ideal home interior in minutes, as long as it doesn't cost a fortune to manage.

The idea of guerrilla marketing is to make a lot out of little, by creating an experience that reaches out to people on a personal level and lingers in their memory after. Some authors describe it as buzz marketing and viral marketing.

It's perfect for awareness campaigns in the way it shocks the potential customer into seeing it in front of them long after they've left it behind. This kind of memory arresting awareness is always effective when the potential customer finds themselves about to make a decision on what to buy.

Ideally, guerrilla marketing activities are done in public places such as streets, beaches, malls and parks, or anywhere where they'll draw more attention. I have a few tips for you to follow when setting up your interior design firm's guerrilla marketing strategy.

- **Identify your target audience's special characteristics**. You already know most of these, but identify those that work hand in hand with what you're planning, such as where they usually hang out, what's most likely to surprise them, and the last thing they expect. Also, find out what they might deem offensive.

- **Pick your strategy/angle**. Guerrilla marketing campaigns can go different ways, but always toward the main goal of creating a different level of awareness and interaction with your design business.

    This is where you determine the angle you need. Buzz and viral content are both good ways to start, but you can also go for ambush marketing, which involves maximising the publicity of an ongoing event to promote your own products.

    There's stealth marketing and a ton of others too. Your budget and the expected goal will be the main determinants.

- **Create an awesome advert**. This is the highlight of the whole campaign. Your success depends on how imaginative, thoughtful and memorable your advert will be. Remember to be unconventional without being offensive or breaking area laws.

- **Confirm the cost, ROI, location and other specificities**. The main reason for choosing guerrilla tactics is that they cost less than traditional marketing methods. During your planning stage, factor in any cost you might incur.

If the costs trump your expected revenue by a large margin, try other alternatives. Speaking of revenue, the Return on Investment from guerrilla marketing is not measured in terms of received orders or short-term profits made only.

There's a lot more to consider, and the ROI can manifest itself in different ways, such as hikes on traffic to your website, higher signup numbers for your newsletter, more calls to your office and more.

Circling back to cost, remember to factor in the cost of a failed marketing campaign, including how to minimise damage (because anything can happen).

- **Plan the follow-up strategy**. Remember I mentioned how guerrilla campaigns do well with awareness and memory? Well, all that adds up to nothing if you don't follow it up with the next step - which is getting people to actually get in touch with you.

So, what if people now know your interior design business after seeing the small well-designed replica houses you were throwing out from a hot air balloon in your town's Main Street?

You risk having them kept in nurseries as toys for toddlers if you don't follow up with another marketing move.

Plan this move ahead – it could be cold calling or asking people to get furniture fittings for the toy houses from your offices - and be ready to tweak it if the guerrilla campaign doesn't go according to plan.

Promotion Strategies

SEO

As an interior designer you need an online platform, also known as a website, for managing your online presence. That website needs to be found easily by potential clients.

In the good old days, when online marketing and advertising weren't so popular, all anyone needed to do was create a website, put some content on it and hope that it would be found by those who need it.

Today, with the internet harbouring hundreds of millions of active websites, that strategy is dead in the water. This is where SEO and paid ads come in. For now, let's discuss SEO.

When you search a particular term, you get pages and pages of search results. The way the results are ordered is not random or a coincidence. It's down to SEO, Search Engine Optimization.

Search Engine Optimization involves improving the ranking of your website in various search results that you haven't paid for (technically these are called 'organic results').

There are various ways you can go about it. One of the most popular ways is text optimization which involves creating your content in such a manner that search engines and people are easily able to make out that your website includes content related to certain search terms (technically these are called 'keywords').

Here's a quick example: Say you've created an interior design website with a special blog dedicated to helping people with their apartment design problems.

Potential keywords can be anything from *'interior designers in Cook County'* to *'How to design your first apartment like a pro'* to just plain *'interiors'*, depending on what you think your target audience will use as search keywords when typing into a browser.

> **I've always explained to my clients in no uncertain terms that it's no use having a website on the internet if it's not going to appear on the first page of search results.**

Internet visitors are not the kindest or the most patient of people, so you can't guarantee that they'll always run over to the next page just to find it.

SEO works in such a way that when your potential visitors finally make a search that closely correlates with some of the keywords you've used, your website shoots to the first page of those search results (ceteris paribus, that is, all factors constant).

Unless your website is the only one of its kind on the internet, SEO is the ultimate determinant of its long or short-term survival.

SEO for your interior design website requires a professional touch. If you're on a tight budget, you can try basic SEO techniques on your own. Nonetheless, it's a lot of continuous work, so you might find yourself giving up and losing your edge.

Somewhere else on the internet, other webmasters will be gearing up to take your hard-earned position in the search results. That's why I always suggest seeking the services of a professional.

YouTube

Video ads are also a major option today. According to Inc. magazine, over 75% of web visitors visit a brand's website after seeing a branded video. That a good number, especially when you consider the thousands of distractions a viewer is faced with before they get to your website.

YouTube ads have made video ads the big deal they are today. You've most likely seen them already. They always play before your favourite video starts, sometimes with an option to skip after 5 seconds. I always suggest YouTube ads to my clients for brand awareness, channel visibility and new announcements.

The millions of viewers YouTube receives every day are its biggest attraction, rendering it the second largest search engine on the internet.

Some of its attributes also provide valuable insight for advertisers, especially the ability to target a specific market based on age, gender, location, demographics, interests etc.

There is also an option for segmenting according to the type of device the viewer is using and the contextual keywords potential clients might use while searching for a video.

YouTube gives you a number of ad options, including display ads, skippable ads, non-skippable ads, **sponsored cards**(which appear like a teaser for a few seconds and generally include content that appears in the video),**overlay ads**(YouTube in-video overlay ads appear across the bottom of a video on watch pages). Because of their visual nature, all of them are good for advertising for you as an interior designer.

Your ad has to;
- Get to the point in 5 seconds or less before people can skip it.
- Be of high quality, because poor quality ads are easily rejected by the algorithm in favour of better-quality ads.
- Be catchy enough for easier recall and to clock higher watch times. The more memorable it is, the more viewers are likely to remember it and refer it to others.

- Leave a clear call to action and links to where viewers can find your online presence after the ad is over.

Homemade YouTube ads are the easiest to spot and even easier to skip. You can of course create your own ad content. But I feel you should get a video agency to help you for optimal results as far as YouTube ads are concerned.

Make sure they use the most relevant keywords such that it is seen by your exact target audience and draws in more conversions.

AdWords Ads

Remember I mentioned paid ads while discussing online marketing and advertising? AdWords is Google's program to manage paid ads.

You might have seen them when browsing the internet. AdWords ads are managed by Google, and appear alongside organic results; the organic search results being results that appear as a result of your SEO efforts.

Google uses an algorithm to display AdWords ads to only the individuals that are most likely to be interested in them, making them a perfect advertising platform.

This is how they work. When internet users make a search request in a browser, ads that are closely related to the search results are displayed all around the organic search results, the organic search results being of course the results that occur naturally, as a result of SEO, and not those you have paid for.

A search for *'commercial interior designers in Delhi'* will bring organic search results on the topic, but also three or four related AdWords ads alongside those organic results.

That seems intrusive, but which form of advertising isn't? AdWords ads have been favourably reviewed by former users and SEO experts, with most opining them to resulting high ROI numbers in comparison to other promotion strategies.

Interior designers can use to great effect. I have always recommended using AdWords ads as long as they are worked right.

If badly implemented, they won't generate returns thereby leaving you with non-performing sunken investments. If you can implement them correctly, they can yield multi-fold returns. Your returns depend on how well you can set them up.

During set up, you determine whether you'll want your ad to be charged based on the impressions, views or click through rate it gets. You'll also set the daily budget, for which you have to set a budget that isn't too low or too high.

Then you have to choose the keywords that Google should look out for when placing your ads. Choosing them requires thinking deeply about your target clients' location, needs and wants.

You also determine the actual words/copy that your ad will use. Will your ad shout out a limited time discount or coolly announce your list of services?

The overall goal is to ensure that your ad is clicked on and visitors get to your website, also known as lead. It's a whole lot of trial and error; you're not always expected to get it right the first time. However, don't worry. As difficult as it sounds, you won't mess it up beyond repair.

Many interior designers I know create and run AdWords campaigns on their own. They research keywords (backlinko.com/google-keyword-planner), determine their ad budgets and analyse their metrics on a daily basis. They also visit informational websites to learn more about the process.

Most of my former clients in this position have highlighted metric analysis as the hardest part of the process. Numbers from an ad campaign are useless unless you can decipher what they mean.

Sometimes, they are a call for a major tweak in the campaign strategy. Sometimes, they are a sign of big leaps made. Sometimes, huge numbers are just temporary. If you find yourself in this situation, you might find it wise to consider professional help.

Facebook Ads

Facebook has long been the go-to platform for social media ads for almost any event or business. Buffer's State of the Social report for 2018 showed that 94% of businesses have already invested in advertising on Facebook. That number alone highlights how popular the platform is.

Recent tweaks to the algorithm that determines what appears on a user's Newsfeed have affected the amount of viewership content from publishers and businesses gets. But it hasn't affected the ads people see. In other words, Facebook ads are still going strong.

I always recommend Facebook ads for brand awareness, visibility and lead generation. Perhaps the best way to start advertising on Facebook is by boosting (you'll notice an option to 'Boost Post' at the lower right hand corner of your post) an existing post you have created on your business's Facebook page.

You can either boost a post among your friends or you can set target demographics among whom your post will be boosted.

Let's look at Facebook ad types. The platform has created a varying set of ad types that cover various purposes well enough.

You get to choose from carousel ads, sponsored mentions, dynamic ads, domain ads (these redirect to your website), video ads, offer ads and more.

Carousel ads show your work through a series of images. They are best used byproduct-oriented businesses, but you can always employ them to showcase your diverse range of services.

Domain ads are perfect for lead generation and future retargeting purposes because clicking on them directly takes visitors to your website.

Video ads are a good choice, especially for future retargeting purposes. Make sure to keep them short and true to your brand. Interior design businesses tend to have a clear, stand-out aesthetic that's distinctly clean, trendy and stylish. I recommend using **offer ads** although I find them quite limiting in who can use them.

> Starting a Facebook campaign is pretty easy. Managing one is not.

That's why some designers I know spend over $6000 in ad spend over 2 months and get 2 new paying gigs while others spend less than $500 and bag 10 new paying clients.

It's not just about looking at big numbers and assuming that you're taking a step forward. You need to look deeper than the metrics to determine whether your budget is paying off and your chosen target audience is converting as expected.

If it's not, you need to work out how to tweak the ad campaign. That's why you should look into a Social Media Manager to handle your Facebook campaigns.

Keep these tips in mind when working on your Facebook ad campaign.

- **Target like a pro**. The power of Facebook ads is in how specific they can be when you're choosing who to advertise to. Look at the information you created about your target clients.

  Now base on that information when choosing the interests, demographics, location and other attributes that will define your ad campaign.

- **Take advantage of retargeting based on the profiles** and demographics you get from the analytics dashboard. Retargeting is very important because you direct these ads at people who expressed interest in your work but didn't get around to booking a consultation. Targeting that audience specifically can reap rich dividends.

- **Use professional images**. Poor images stand out almost immediately so avoid them. Make sure the colour palette of the photos matches your brand too. That way, your ad will speak to your audience and capture their interest.

- **Understand your potential clients and create ads in languages they understand.** Go for ad copy that entertains while telling your message the way your target audience would like to hear it.

Bachelor Jack Barr may not be enthused much by an ad that's written more for John and Jack, the gay couple living in an apartment.

- **Check each ad's analytics in real time and remember** to look at the metrics that matter most such as leads, reach and engagement, depending on your current goal. Facebook gives you a lot of data on your ad campaigns. It's important to choose the data set that reveals how well your campaign is doing.

- **Structure your ads to go live optimally, i.e.** when you most expect your audience to be using Facebook. You can easily do that with a third party service like Buffer.

Quora Ads

A few years ago, Quora ads weren't a thing. But the platform was already popular, so when their self-served feature (a self-serve ad is one which is served to viewers by the advertiser themselves, without involving a salesperson) was released worldwide in 2017, it quickly became a popular way to run ads.

If you hadn't heard of Quora before now, it's one of, if not the, most popular Q&A platform in the world right now with over 300 million monthly unique visitors from all over the globe as of last reporting (searchengineland.com/quora-introduces-broad-targeting-says-audience-hits-300-million-monthly-users-305517).

The attraction is in the professionalism of the answers given on the platform, some of which come from world known experts and celebrities. Some very difficult and sensitive questions that people may not like to ask in person are answered on Quora.

Ads on Quora are of two main types; personal promotion and regular ads.

Personal promotion involves answering a question and promoting yourself in the answer by linking to your website or other online channels. That is what everyone was doing before the ad system was released.

But like with anything that's been overdone, this form of promotion is worn out. I only recommend using it with a strategy in mind. The strategy requires that you position yourself as an expert on the issue you're answering such that readers looking for answers can learn to expect value from you.

With this strategy, longer, more detailed but equally relevant answers are preferred to the quick, much short pieces that everyone writes. The more answers you write, the higher your reputation, ranking and answer views.

A few tips to get personal promotion right:

Place links to your website/other channels only when it's relevant. The link should not be seen to be forcibly placed there.
Do NOT place the link to your website too early on in the answer.
Remember, you may be advertising yourself but the person reading your answer is primarily looking for an informative answer.
Place links to other websites as well to ensure your answer looks professional. Website is the best from of address you can create online for your interior design business.

Creating and running an advert campaign is the other option. Like Facebook and other social platforms, Quora now allows you to run ads on their platforms. The first Quora ads were not as attractive as Facebook ads but things are getting better.

Nowadays they are placed non-intrusively between answers to a question. I recommend Quora ads for designers because;

- They are easy to set up and manage. The dashboard is as easy to use as Facebook's.

- They have cheaper leads than most of the other platforms. A couple of clients that recently took up Quora ads have reported less spending on cost per lead than with AdWords and Facebook.

- You can target your ads better. You can select a target audience based on questions asked, locations (based on zip code), topics of interest and platforms (desktop or mobile).

- They provide more detailed analytics on conversions, ad spend, impressions, delivery and cost per click in real time.

- They are exposed to high-quality traffic unlike most ads on the internet because of the nature of Quora and how targeted they can be.

Direct targeting is the golden sauce here too. Always remember, your objective is to create content that will appeal to your target clients. It follows that when you select your audience on Quora, you should use the attributes you gave your target clients (go back to chapter 5 for a quick brush-up in case you don't follow).

Would they even have a need for the platform or know about it?

As with any platform you publish content on, please remember to check out Quora's advertising guidelines first. There are a strict set of rules regarding headings, word count per section, punctuation and wordplay.

Just like Google, Quora uses the bidding system for its ads. Remember to make a higher bid at the check-in auction to rise above the competition. When your ad goes live, it competes with hundreds of other ads for the same spots on the page. According to Quora, the top spot is won by the ad that places the highest bid.

A higher bid for your ad will result in a lower overall cost. Tests done by the good folks over at *MarketingLand* found that bidding higher results in higher CTRs and lower CPCs, which is the perfect way to go.

Don't forget to set up your Conversion Pixel for the Quora ad; you need it to track each website conversion as it happens.

Partnering Up with Real Estate Agents and Builders

This is another particularly helpful tactic that I've employed myself in the past. It's also one of the easiest ways of promoting yourself and getting your first clients.

Here's how it works:
You partner with other service providers in your industry especially those that the members of your target audience would also need.

In this case, they would be architects, builders, real estate salesmen, plumbers, painters and the like. You then refer each other when you get clients.

Some partnerships can be made for all such that there is sharing of profits at the end of the day, but that's quite complex. Other partnerships work on commission basis, where you pay a small fee for each client referred to you by another business.

The beauty of referral partnerships is that you have created a complete ecosystem that will meet most of the needs a client might have.

Think about it from the client's point of view.

Say you're a client with two jobs - a plumbing job and a design job. You're naturally looking through the phone book, asking people and searching online. Finally, you get a plumber who does a good job. AND the plumber tells you he knows a designer who can get your design job done.

Wouldn't that put you in a good mood? Wouldn't you refer them to your friends? Wouldn't you ask them for suggestions when you have a plumbing job?

Once you can create this kind of a network, stretching across industry verticals, you'll find it easier to get clients.

How to get started:

- **Look up the addresses** and other contact information of other service providers related to housing and interior design. That could be anyone from a random house painter to a well-known architect. You can also find such information in trade magazines and on their websites.

- **Schedule a meeting** with them and lay out your plans. Some people are less formal, so you can meet them at social events and ask them to refer to you just like you refer to them.

  Be ready to agree to a commission-based system in case you're dealing with top service providers. Plus, leave a couple of contact documents with them, like business cards.

- For each client you're referred, **do the necessary research**. It's important that you absolutely dazzle them when you meet. Research includes technical knowledge so you can give them an idea of what their proposed job involves, an idea of the supplies market so you can draw up an estimate and an honest assessment of what kind of time you need to complete the work.

  Remember, the network you've taken pains to grow will drop you once clients start complaining that your work is sub-standard.

  If you think going all the way to their business premises to strike partnerships with them will be hard for you, there is an alternative.

You can keep track of the jobs other service providers are doing. The objective is to understand the overall jobs that are in the market, where interior design fits in and which clients need interior design services.

Armed with that knowledge, you can send a sales pitch to the people who your research reveals to be in need of your services. Of course, this requires that you possess the necessary technicals to get that data from the internet. And your sales pitch needs to be carefully crafted to appeal to the target client.

Pinterest

This is a big platform for interior designers because of its visual set up and board cataloguing feature. It's perfect for brand awareness and lead acquisition.

While it isn't one of the bigger platforms for advertising, the fact that it allows you to share images of your completed projects, works in progress and yourself at work (humanising yourself) is a good way to draw eyeballs.

Pinterest users create boards on which they can save 'pins' they've found on the platform or anywhere else on the internet. Businesses like yours can create boards too on which you share your images and allow them to be seen by other Pinterest users.

Boards created by users literally become mini museums for your work and they can be shared right across the internet, spreading the word further. Just make sure you use the best images possible.

Webinars and Podcasts

Webinars and podcasts are another marketing medium that I recommend you embrace.

Each one of them is a good starting platform for projecting your authority, expertise and knowledge on various issues, especially your interior design niche. Podcasts tend to have smaller though highly dedicated listeners/viewers.

Webinars attract niche specific individuals who are looking for a solution to a problem or a new technique of doing things. Both podcasts and webinars also come with one added benefit; you can start your own if you can't find any that suits your niche or standard.

Here's a plan I recommend to get started.

For podcasts:

Look for available interior design podcasts in your region or country. You can find them on popular podcast platforms such as Stitcher or iTunes, or from industry websites, trade journal recommendations and trade magazine reviews.

Sieve through for the good ones and compatibility. Not every podcast is commendable. Some are outright horrible. But niche podcasts aren't very common, especially podcasts on interior design.

Look for those that are hosted near you, maybe in a neighbouring city. Look out for those with high listenership. Look out for those that would speak to your target audience.

Pitch them for your presence. Most podcasts allow potential guests onto the show, but you have to pitch what you'll talk about first.

Make sure your pitch highlights how much value you'll give listeners and not how much you'll talk about yourself. Make sure your pitch fits the style of their podcast.

When you get onto the show, offer valuable advice and project your authority without coming off as showy. **Only talk about your services when your host invites you to.**

NB: Additionally, you can strike marketing arrangements with podcasts you think have the listenership that needs your designer services. Ideally, it should be a commission-based contract, with a certain percentage given to the podcast for each listener converted into a buyer of your services.

For webinars
- Look out for future industry webinars and see how you can get involved.
- Sign up for them, and if you can, ask to be a speaker (especially if they are local webinars). Just like podcasts, make sure your pitch matches their style.
- When given a chance to speak, concentrate on offering advice. Refer to your own service only when the host asks you to.

Many people get stage fright when speaking at a public forum for the first time. While that's completely natural, it's also natural to not get invited back if you mumble or stutter too much. Or if you speak too rapidly.

Tip: When and if any of the methods above proves difficult for you, there's always a way out: Start your own webinar or podcast.

Website
By now you've noticed that all the promotion strategies discussed above require an online presence of some sort.

The starting point for any online presence is a website. That website becomes your online storefront because that's where potential clients check when considering hiring you.

You also keep your work portfolios and contact info there. Simply put, a website is very, very important. Your website must **POP**. That calls for professional design.

I always suggest that my clients seek out professional website design services rather than do it themselves because it's just better. Professional web designers know what you need and how to get there.

I know there are platforms like WIX that help you design your own website by just dragging and dropping, but it's not the easiest process. The chances of getting stuck midway are higher than the chances of creating a full-blown website on your own.

If you're looking for a professional website, there are more advanced design requirements that only a professional would know. Still, if you are on a low budget, a free WordPress website is a good start.

Basic website design is a breeze and you can always do it yourself.

However, to get your website ready for SEO and to maximize the chances of converting visitors into clients, you should get a trained professional to design your website.

Searchmetry does offer a well-rounded website design service but they are fully booked. You can get on the waiting list by emailing them at a@searchmetry.com

✶ CHAPTER TAKEAWAYS ✶

- ✓ You need to market your business. Doesn't matter if you're dealing with a smaller audience or not selling physical products.

- ✓ Sometimes, you need guerrilla marketing to get your point across. Just make sure you don't break regional laws or scare people.

- ✓ Social media platforms are the new *'gold'*. Don't let Instagram, Twitter, Facebook, Pinterest and other social platforms pass you by.

- ✓ Retargeting is important since you're trying to tip fence-sitters over into booking a consult.

- ✓ You need a website for your business. Get one immediately.

- ✓ Smaller media platforms like podcasts and webinars can be good alternatives to the pricier and grander traditional methods when it comes to promoting yourself and your business.

- ✓ However much you like direct marketing, do NOT ignore indirect marketing. Project yourself as an authority who provides answers to people. Clients will start trickling in naturally.

CHAPTER 7:

Pricing Your Services for Profit

In this section, we explore the different ways you can price your interior design services.

For interior designers, pricing services has always presented a few challenges.

Interior designers usually prefer one of the methods below to price their services. Each of them is worth considering - as I have learned from years of alternating between them for projects - but I have also found that they each have faults that designers should be wary of.

Here's a simple analysis of each method.

Pricing Per Hour

You, the designer, set a specific fee to be charged per hour, the same way most professionals charge for their services across countries like the United States.

You should give the client a proper estimate of how difficult the job is and base your per hour fee on that.

Alternatively, you can follow the industry's 'per hour' range in your location. At the end of the project, the total number of hours spent on the project are counted and billed in terms of the per hour fee you set to create a total sum.

i.e. *$50 (your fee per hour) × 720 (hours spent working on a project, averaging 12 hours a day for 2 months = $36, 000 (total fees charged)*

On paper, this method sounds error proof. But I have seen its downsides. I agree that for a starting designer, and for smaller projects, the hourly charge system can save both parties a lot of paperwork and time.

But, in most cases, and usually on bigger projects, clients tend to feel like they're being cheated by the per hour system. Some actually end up requesting evidence of how each hour was spent.

Needless to say this can eat up time that you spend documenting exactly what you're doing; time you'd rather spend designing.

Moreover, such disputes can spill over, leading to arguments and lawsuits that will harm your reputation and possibly reduce the sum of money you actually get at the end of it all while saddling you with legal costs.

Using a Flat Rate/Prefixed Rate

With this method, your role as a designer is to work out a good estimate of what you believe you're worth for a specific project and then set a flat fee. The fee can be anything from less than $3000 to more than $50, 000.

The difference here is that there is no increase in remuneration for you even when the project takes up more time than expected, or requires more resources. The flat rate usually covers only your fee as a designer; you are still provided with finances for sourcing and purchasing decoration pieces.

The flat rate method has worked for a number of my clients, and most have highlighted its power to boost their incomes during periods of low work. Most admitted that it made them appear affordable enough to be hired, which wouldn't have worked with an accumulative remuneration system like the per hour method.

But they also noted that while it got them hired, it also exposed them to the danger of undercharging for their services, especially when the projects turned out more complex or longer running than expected.

Charging A Percentage of the Entire Budget (15-30%)

This is a system I wholeheartedly recommend. The client can't dispute anything because the budget is drawn up in black and white. On the other hand, the budget is a pretty good approximation of the complexity of the project so you earn a fair fee. If the work runs longer than you expected, the budget will need to be hiked and your remuneration will rise in lockstep.

In calculation, you cover every aspect of the design process right from consultation to drafting to design to installations. Once the total budget is drawn up, your fee is determined by that figure.

You set the percentage. It could be anything from 10 – 30%.
i.e. *total cost of the whole design project from start to finish = $50,000*
designer's pay is 20% of total cost = 20% × $50,000 = $10,000

So, the client will pay a total of $60,000 for your vision, plans and the actual materialization of the vision.

This method is particularly good for large projects, where even a smaller percentage can result in a good payday. But for smaller projects, it might pose a few issues.

On the one hand, the client may not be able to bear a 30% or even 15% extra expense on your services. On the other hand, you may be disappointed by your own income - for example a $10000 budget will yield a $3000 fee which you may not be satisfied with.

Percentage Over Costs + Small Design Commission

This method is still hugely popular among interior designers today, and for good reason. Here, you get paid a small fee as your design commission, but your major fee comes from a percentage mark-up on all the goods you purchase for the design project (such as the furniture and lighting and fabrics).

You and the client agree on the mark-up percentage within your binding agreement.
i.e. *Total cost of items purchased for the project = $25,000*
total percentage mark-up at 20% = 20% × $25,000 = $5000

so, total pay for designer would be;
$500 (design commission) + $5000 (mark-up) = $5500

As with the percentage method, on smaller projects, this method might not work out well for your bank account. It can also sow discord if the client assumes you are purposefully purchasing expensive furnishings to boost your own mark-up and ultimate pay packet.

Costing per square meter/feet
For interior designers in commercial real estate, this has always been the go-to method for service pricing.

It's pretty straightforward too; a fee is set to be charged per square ft. (or appropriate regional unit of measurement) for the whole length and breadth of the rooms to be covered.

i.e. in the case of interior design for three rooms (140 sq. ft, 200 sq. ft and 300 sq. ft) at a set design charge of $20 per square foot.

*= $20 * (140 + 200 + 300) sq. ft = $12,800*

As I noted above, this method is ideal for commercial projects, because the square foot system is preferred there. It also works well for new spaces. **For residential and other types of projects, this method might not be a good choice.**

Charging Per Hour + Markup on Goods Purchased

This is another variation on the 'percentage markup method on purchases' system. Here, you capture both elements - a per hour charge to reflect your labour and a markup on purchases to reflect the complexity of the project.

i.e. designer's charge per hour = $35
total number of hours worked = 720
percentage mark-up on purchases = 10%
total cost of purchases = $10,000

designer's total pay = ($35 × 720) + (10% × $10,000) = $26,200

As you might have noticed, this method racks up quite a figure for the designer.

However, it's not very popular with clients because it appears to them like you're double charging.

I recommend negotiating with the client and arriving at a reasonable figure - one that makes you feel your labour is respected and the client feel that they're getting a good deal.

Retail Charging

In this system, the client does not directly pay you anything. Instead, you negotiate a 'designer's discount' from the supplier of furnishings. That is, you negotiate with the seller of furnishings to buy the materials required in your project at a discount. But the client pays the face value of the furnishings. The discount becomes your fee.

i.e. *total displayed cost of various items from one shop = $10,000*
The client pays you $10,000 to procure the items.
designer's discount offered = 20% = 20% × $10,000 = $2000
actual price at which you buy the items then becomes = $10,000 - $2000 = $8000

your pay is = $10,000 (cost of items in shop) – $8000 (actual price at which you but it after the discount) = $2000

At the end of the day, your pay is directly equal to your designer's discount. That figure is discussed between you and the shop only sans the client, and so you directly determine your pay.

You might see it already that, you're only going to get a high pay using this method when dealing with rare, vintage or very expensive items. Such items can always command a good discount. Smaller everyday items tend to be cheaper already, so your discount is likely to be lower. In that case your pay size will depend on the amount of material you're procuring.

This method also fails to consider other aspects of the design process that you're involved in. You're more likely to end up nearly working for free.

The other disadvantage of this method is the same as that of the proportional billing system - the client may suspect you're buying costlier materials to inflate your own paycheck.

Charging for Creating a Vision and A Design Plan Only

In some cases, clients handle the purchase and installation of design items themselves. Only the creation of the vision and the design plans is left to the interior designer.

This work format can be priced using any of the **non-percentage** markup methods listed above. Personally, I'd recommend per hour or flat rate billing in this situation.

A combination of the above – I RECOMMEND

At the end of the day, all the methods above are ideal for only specific situations. That's why I recommend always being prepared to apply all of them (for example have a discount pre-negotiated with a supplier and so on) so that you can combine different methods on a single project.

- For **small and medium residential projects**, I recommend using a combination of the flat rate (for consultation services) and 'per hour' for any physical work you do, or just using a plain fixed rate. Usually, these two alternatives fit well with clients looking to complete small interior design projects.

- For **commercial projects and huge residential projects,** I recommend using a combination of the flat rate method (for consultation services) and 'per square foot' method when working with the space, or a combination of a design commission (this will include the consultation fee) and a percentage markup on items purchased.

- For **big, complex projects**, I recommend that you break up the design process intro stages, starting with consultation, planning and design, down to buying of items and installation. And think which method would work the best for each step. Finally, make sure you explain your billing plan clearly to the client.

Remember the following;

At the end of the day, the client determines the budget for their project; you either go along with it or pass it up.

If you believe a slight increase in the budget would lead to better results, you can pass it on to the client. The client then decides whether or not to change their budget allotments.

Make a point of meeting up with the client first and going over the project details. In preparation for these meetings, get information on the current pricing of the different items that may be needed for the project.

This information should back up your proposed total spend on the project and relieve the client of any worry that they might get cheated in the process. You should also state your expected remuneration for the project, how you're going to bill the client and explain to them why it's fair.

All of this ends up in the work agreement you sign with the client. It's important that you get templates of work agreements for interior designers before you draw up your own.

Structuring Your Total Fee

The fee you get paid as an interior designer directly depends on a few factors – your expertise, your stature as a designer, your past work and more. Ideally, you should have a basic in mind for your fee, even before you go out looking for gigs. Your fee should be comprised of;

1. A consultation fee

This fee can be determined per hour or as a flat rate, but should cover the time and effort you spend discussing the project with the client whether or not you are eventually hired to work fully on the project.

Many designers make a mistake of not charging for these hours and efforts, and that undercuts their total pay at day's end.

2. A work fee

This is the fee you negotiate with the client following any of the pricing methods discussed earlier. It covers every aspect of your efforts on the project, right from sketching to purchasing of items.

* What the heck? Didn't I just say you should fit the billing system with the job? Then why am I saying you should have a structure in mind before you start looking for gigs?

No, I am not contradicting myself.

What I'm saying here is that you should have a separate fee for consultation and a separate fee for physical work for most projects. And you should plan accordingly.

When you receive an actual project, you determine whether it's a very small project by your standards or a very complicated one and adjust your fee structure accordingly. It always helps to have a starting position and then work your way up (or down) depending on the circumstances.

As you become more experienced and grow your company, you can also add **a retainer fee** to your total fee. Retainers are commonly exercised by highly sought-after professionals in almost every industry, and they are legal.

Note: As you structure your designer fees, remember to factor in costs like taxes and costs because they need to be covered for you to make any profit off of your work.

✶ CHAPTER TAKEAWAYS ✶

- ✓ There's no set pricing formula for interior design services. Rather, there are many different ways you can go, depending on the project in question.

- ✓ The best pricing strategy to combine the various billing systems judiciously. That gives you the scope to bill the client for all the work - whether consultative or physical - that you do for them while also satisfying the client that they're being billed fairly according to the difficulty of their project.

- ✓ Remember to consider your consultation time when pricing your service. Charge for it separately along with the actual design or decorating work.

- ✓ Remember to look ahead when deciding on the fees you charge, Sometimes, charging lower is good if you believe doing so will open more doors for you after completion.

CHAPTER 8:

Modern Web Design for Interior Designers

Today, having a web presence is no longer just an option. With millions of people visiting Google and other search engines every day for help and answers, it pays to have an address online so you too will appear on search engines' results pages via your website.

> **A website is the best identity you can give your interior design business online.**

Websites come in many forms and types. There's no one-size-fits-all website template I can recommend; I believe that an interior designer's website must be designed in line with their identity.

In this section, we look at how you can set up your website professionally, including all the features it must have AND how to create content for them.

First, **create a plan**. What will the purpose of your website be, apart from being your online address? What do you want visitors to your websites to do after browsing through your website? That's the motive you need to know beforehand.

Websites can be built for any number of reasons. Some are created for mere display of products. Others are created to directly sell them.

Some companies create websites to enable people to understand more about their services. Such websites usually have a range of motives, such as checking out a demo of the services or requesting an appointment.

In your case, your website should be created with the main motive of **enabling people to request an appointment or a call back**. That motive will directly determine how your call-to-action buttons will read (Think of '**Request an appointment**" "**Get in touch with me directly**" rather than '**Sign Up**' or '**Buy Now**').

That way, you can expect the people that visit your website to call your business and ask about your services. You can also measure how your website is performing in terms of the difference between the number of people visiting the website versus those that are calling.

Once you have your plan and your motive, the next step is to **build your website's major sections**.

The major sections:

A Portfolio

As an interior designer, you probably already have your portfolio in place. People need to be able to see that portfolio on your website to convince them you can meet their expectations.

Your portfolio is a pretty big factor in whether visitors to your website think it's worthwhile booking a consultation with you. And people's attention span online isn't that big. So, you need to absolutely dazzle them at first glance. It's Go Big or Go Home.

What to Include in Your Portfolio

Don't get confused about what to or not to add in your portfolio. There is basic information that a visitor or potential client needs to see as they browse through the portfolio.

That is the information I always have my clients include and display visibly. I recommend the following to be part of your basic information:

- Your name
- A short bio about yourself (talking about your aesthetic as a designer in summary)
- A profile picture of your design business's logo (the one you created in an earlier section)
- A link to your online platforms (YouTube, Pinterest, Facebook, Instagram etc.)
- You should also add;

- Photos of finished projects
- FF&E schedules
- CAD drawings

How to Make Your Portfolio Stand Out

Here's a fact: every major interior designer has their portfolio on their website, including your niche competitors. Even the ones who may have started out just a couple of months before you did will have their portfolio in place, I can assure you. To put it bluntly, just having a portfolio will not do.

That's why you need to make your portfolio stand out and capture a visitor's interest the moment they see it.

There are two parts to it. One, the portfolio must contain only that work you truly consider your best. Two, it must be presented attractively. Here's how to achieve that:

1. Sit with your work and client testimonials. Choose only those projects that you feel represent your best work. Then ensure that the testimonials, if any, also speak very highly of those projects. If you feel doubt about a project, skip it. Don't include it just to puff up your portfolio.

2. Start with your most recent work and go backwards in time.

3. All your photos must be high resolution.

4. Choose a colour theme - will you use only black and white or go for full colour? Which has the better effect you're looking for?

5. Make sure your name and bio are visible

6. Pick a striking layout for the photos; I recommend either the grid or the linear layouts but you can be creative; however, remember that the focus needs to remain on your project photos and that the photos must not clash with each other or overlap.

7. Include the source of inspiration for whatever design you created.

8. **Make it about your target client.** Remember, you're not proving your worth to yourself. You're proving it to your client. So ensure that what goes into your portfolio is what your target client would need themselves or would recommend to someone.

Yes, you can include a project or two that the target client may not want but you think is your absolute very best work, but remember to place it at the end. It's there are a kind of implicit testimonial to your design prowess; not as part of your main pitch to your target client.

9. Include your processes in the portfolio too; the background work that results in all those finished images.

   Go on and include sample boards, mood boards, sketches etc. You might also include, on the side, the story of how the project came about, from commissioning stage to submission.

10. With each slide, highlight what you're good at by showing more samples of it. Make sure that each slide highlights your various design abilities, whether it's working with contrast colours, channelling an era or following a theme.

11. Each slide should have a clear label of what the image is about. That should also include a short, catchy description that's quick to read and easy to understand.

12. Most importantly, **keep it brief**. Photos of your work might be great, but one can only view so much without seeing sudden faults, making assumptions or feeling tired. If that happens, the visitor is prone to leave your website.

13. That's why you should keep the online portfolio down to **10 -20** slides at a time. Each slide contains an image. If you want to add a project to the portfolio make sure you remove an older one.

Your 'About-Me' Page

Most visitors to interior design websites are interested in the designer or the firm behind the website. So, they are more than likely to check out the 'About' page.

In other words, your 'About-Me' page is important.

The 'About' page section does more than just talk about you; it establishes a connection between you and a visitor and **convinces them to call you**. How? Because after the visitor has perused your site, they may need a final push into booking a consultation with you.

They seek answers to questions like *"His work is great, but is he our type?"*, *"Would he understand our needs?"* or *"Where is she located anyway? I like her work but she could be too far out of town."*

It can also be more specific questions like *"What's his take on Scandinavian design?"* or purchase-decision-determinant musings like *"Let's see how expensive this one is."* Your 'About' page must answer these questions to their satisfaction.

Once it does, you, my dear, will have bagged them. Expect a stream of phone calls, or at least a bookmark in their browser. Or maybe a Pin Up of one of your portfolio images on their *'Future Home Renovations'* board on Pinterest.

If it doesn't answer these questions though, you lose the connection. They go on to another interior designer's website that Google recommended (it could be the guy that was 5 results below in the search rankings, imagine that!).

Of course, sometimes, your 'About' page is the sieve you need to weed out clients that don't fit well into your target market. They won't get your vibe. But most of the time, that one page marks the thin red line between getting and losing that wonderful client who may have as many as 10 gigs lined up.

Almost all website templates I've seen come with the 'About' page section already installed. Those that don't tend to have a widget that enables you to add one or change its position.

But in any case, at the beginning, the 'About' page is always just a blank slate. You have to fill it up with content.

Your 'About-Me' page must:
- Include your businesses' who, what, where and how.
- Have a good, short bio that spells out who your target clients are and what you do for them. It should also highlight how you got into the business.

Side Note: Just like in the movies, a touch of emotion is always a good addition to your story. It helps forge a connection with readers. To that end it.
- Must have images of you and your team at work.

Should answer the following questions;
- Which companies or individuals have you worked for in the past?
- Any statistics about your business? Awards maybe? (People just love numbers so much)
- What are your design influences?
- Any high-profile endorsements from public figures?

- What's your process?
- What makes you different from other designers?

In summary, your "About page should, through photos and text, explain how you operate, what your values are, what your mission is and give the visitor an all-round idea of who you are.

Your 'Services' Page

This is literally your online storefront. The services on this page are what people are ultimately looking for when they browse your website.

Don't confuse potential clients by placing your services on too many pages or using some crazy layout fad. All that just detours clients off of the road to booking a consultation with you.

Combine all your services onto one main page and make sure it's listed and clearly visible on the main menu. Explain each service using a short paragraph and mention who might need it.

Make use of Call-to-action buttons like 'Find Out More' at the end of each service to direct potential clients further down your marketing funnel. And when they click on the button, make sure they are taken to the Contacts page so that they can call or email you.

Press and Testimonials Section/Page

You might be wondering if you even need press and testimonials. I'll give you the ultimate confirmation – yes you do. People always want to have a third opinion before buying anything just to be sure.

> **Testimonials and press are like reviews on a shopping website because they offer a third opinion.**

And there's proof of their effectiveness. Studies done on the power of reviews show that more than 90% of consumers consider customer reviews before making a purchase decision. Think about that.

Think about the number of potential clients you're likely to lose every day because you lack a testimonial or press mention to quiet their last-minute doubts.

Getting Testimonials

You can't force your local newspaper to write for you, so I'll offer help on how to get testimonials for your website. I always suggest the following ways and they've always worked for my clients.

Use submission forms on your website. It can be at the end of the testimonials page, or it could be a random button with, say 'Leave a review' positioned strategically all over the website.

Requesting them from every client whose project you complete. This is pretty straightforward. You've provided them a service and you're asking them to make an assessment of how good your work is.

Use follow up emails. Assuming you got the email of every client that you worked for, a follow up email is always a good non-intrusive way to get them to leave a review.

Make some calls. Sometimes, calling people and reminding them to leave that review they promised is the best move forward.

How to Make Your Testimonials and Press Mentions Stand Out

Because they are part of the website content, your hard-earned testimonials and press mentions might be easily missed by the very people they are displayed for.

That's essentially why you have to make sure they stand out too. You can try the following tricks:

- Use a separate background for them.

- Use different text for them than the rest of the website

- Try unique text formatting for them only. You could make them italic, bold, left aligned etc.

- Try aligning each testimonial with a photograph of its owner. That's a double win, for credibility and for eye grabbing purposes.

- Use video testimonials alongside text testimonials. These ones are good for credibility too.

- Ensure correct placement. This is important. From experience, I've found three options to work best.

    o   On the home page

This is the place almost every new visitor checks out. You ought to place them not very far from the top because some people don't scroll down to the bottom.

Some big company websites place one testimonial at the very top of their home pages so that visitors start browsing with that positive information in mind.

- On a separate page/section of their own

This page has to be accessible from the main menu, probably marked 'Testimonials' for good measure. This alternative works well when the menu is properly designed and easy to use.

The only downside is that only visitors with an interest in testimonials will click on the menu. Others may never notice the button at all.

You can still draw in the doubting Thomas's with a testimonial placed randomly on your web pages and fitted with a link to the Testimonials page.

- On the services page, alongside the services

This works very well especially if the testimonials correlate with the services being described. Placing the service's description alongside a review of that same service is a smart way of keeping customers in the loop.

With the 'About' page and testimonials out of the way, you should, **start decorating** your website.

Unique Typography

For an interior design website, the typography is more than important. A proper font complements the designer's aesthetic ability seamlessly. Use a not-so-good choice of font and it will stand out like jagged glass all over your website.

Every website comes with a slew of font designs you can employ. If you want better, you can always purchase premium fonts. Make sure you keep fonts consistent in the various sections and don't change them too often. Opt for warmer, shapely fonts that are legible and attractive.

Hero Images

According to *Unbounce*, a hero shot (a hero image) is a visual representation of your offer that demonstrates how your product or service actually works so that your prospective customers can picture themselves using it.

The hero image is essentially the first image – usually a wide banner image covering the first half or more of the computer screen – that visitors get to see. It greets visitors and tells them what your website's about.

Picture digital payment service provider PayPal's website. Their homepage has a series of rotating hero images, usually comprised of 'a random individual that's just received a mobile PayPal payment', 'a young business owner smiling with her PayPal Mastercard with her business in the background' or a satisfied shopper making a PayPal payment.

You can decipher all that by just looking at the photos. They're so aptly placed that even a first-time visitor would easily know what the website was about.

Hero images are usually accompanied with catchy taglines and completed with a button that bears a call to action. In your case, with your motive, your button/call-to-action would range from '**Learn more**' to '**See our Past Work**'.

New website templates usually come with image placeholders for these hero images, so you need to replace them. You can always get good hero images from photography sites like Flickr, Getty Images etc. if you are willing to go the extra mile and pay for them.

Some sites like *Fotolia* and *Pixabay* have free photos you can use. You can also hire a freelance photographer to get some shots for you.

But you can also design your own hero images with online design platforms such as Canva or get ideas from Behance. As a last, desperate attempt, you can take your own photographs.

Your hero image should;

- Be of high quality i.e. good resolutions

- Easily tell a story of what your design firm offers or how you solve design problems, such as how you transform rooms for children of different sexes.

- Speak to your target audience. Right from the start, your target audience should recognise themselves in the hero images.

  PayPal knows that its target audience cuts across to include teens, students and small business owners plus working adults, which explains those rotating images with a representation of each group.

If you are targeting young parents or restaurant owners, a photo depicting a young bachelor sitting in a beautiful living room definitely won't do, regardless of beauty.

- Be simple, not tacky and overcrowded. It should complement your website's beauty and your overall aesthetic.

Background Videos

Since 2010, the demand for video has increased. Video now appears everywhere in various formats. Background videos function like hero images. Their ability to attract a visitor's attention – even for 5 extra seconds - is their biggest selling point.

They have been proven to increase visitor on-site time and click through rate, which can only be a good thing for you. For the best results, your background videos should be short, but still clearly show what your website is about, i.e. your design niche and your target clients.

Design Cards

Note: I've included business card design in this website design section because both are done using software, and both are important for marketing your interior design business.

Visiting cards, better known as business cards, are still an integral part of any interior designer's marketing arsenal today. They drive as much business as any website or print advert in a magazine, so they need to be carefully thought through.

For starters, the old 'plain white paper business card' no longer cuts it. It's been around for too long, and while I don't discredit its abilities, I don't recommend you go for it either.

Being in a creative industry requires that your business card stand out immediately. It's expected of you. The design of your visiting card will be your calling card.

So, what should your business card be like? Unique, striking and professional is the best way to go. Your card should also achieve its task of getting people to call you with ease. How? By being durable and having standout design.

Follow this link (www.searchmetry.com/business-card/designing-business-card) to checkout my extended post on some amazing ideas I recommend for your Interior Designer Business Card.

Hidden Menu

A menu is an important part of navigating a website, but it can also prove distracting for the average visitor. The power of your menu is in how good and helpful it is without being overwhelming.

This always presents a conundrum of sorts; a good menu needs to have enough sections (and subsections if need be) so as to easily direct a visitor. It also mustn't be too long or too wide to cover up valuable website display space.

That's where hidden menus come in. Hidden menus are designed to appear as a single icon on the website whose contents can only be revealed when it's clicked on.

They don't take up website space, leaving visitors to focus on your hero images, calls-to action and text content. You need one such hidden menu for your design website. Don't worry; they are easy to set up. Almost every website today already has one.

Maintain a Blog

I might have placed this last but having a blog on your website is very, very important. The content that you place on the blog helps your website appear in search engine results better.

You can optimize that content to offer solutions that your target audience would look for, such as blog posts on *'How to maintain a house'* or *'How to fight rodents in your basement'* or *'The latest trends in interior design to check out'*.

You can also use some of the content to promote yourself and your services. A blog post in that regard would still be helpful for the reader. It could be *'How to identify the best interior designer for your next project'* or *'Here's what you need for your next interior design project'*.

In the same vein, you could also relate stories from your latest design projects to give readers a mini peek into your world so they can see if you're the real deal.

To complete this 'pseudo-infomercial', remember to direct readers to your portfolio with a link to see some of the photographs from those projects that you just completed.

A blog is also another platform for you to project your authority over your area of expertise by sharing information that provides solutions to problems your target audience is most likely to be facing.

Most website templates come with inbuilt blog sections, so creating one shouldn't be such a problem.

Extra: Add 'Share' Buttons

Crowdsourcing is the new mantra on the block. And 'share' buttons represent crowdsourced publicity for your website. Adding share buttons is pretty easy; as with 'About', the blog, there are settings for just that.

Pro Tip: Ensure your website loads easily.

I've told you to include 'rich content' - high resolution images, videos and so on - to your website. The flip side of it is that it can make your website take time to load. If that happens, viewers are very likely to move to another website without even looking at yours.

So ensure that your website - every single webpage - loads easily. Adjust your content if necessary.

If you feel the content is being degraded too much and is in danger of looking ugly, don't reduce its quality further. Add a message at the very top of the webpage saying 'Please allow a few moments for the images to load'.

✶ CHAPTER TAKEAWAYS ✶

- ✓ A website is absolutely necessary for an interior design business. Don't be told otherwise.

- ✓ If you don't have a portfolio ready, get started on it. A portfolio is like your demo; potential clients need to see it.

- ✓ Make through choices as regards your hero images, your portfolio images, your website colour palette and your typography because they make or break your website.

- ✓ The placement of various features on your website matters immensely. If stuff is hard to find, you're losing.

- ✓ The good old white business cards can still work for your marketing and promotion, but they're way too outdated. Try the newer, smarter looking options.

- ✓ If you can, get that blog running. It can be a video blog, like on YouTube or the usual one via platforms like WordPress. You'll love their SEO benefits.

- ✓ Ensure your website loads easily. If it's a trade-off between some rich content and the webpage taking time to load, side with the webpage and adjust the content to make the webpage load faster.

CHAPTER 9:

Get Discovered with SEO

Imagine this scenario. A potential client Googles *'affordable interior designers in New Delhi'*. Among the search results that are displayed, yours doesn't appear despite you being located in New Delhi and offering the exact kind of solutions he or she is looking for.

There is no mention of you and your practice anywhere, not even on the 3rd page of search results where search results get a bit off script. And this is after you have created a website for your business, lit it up with your logo and portfolio and worked through some of the marketing/promotion methods we talked about earlier.

So, why would it happen to you after all that effort? Wasn't having a website supposed to make your business easy to find on the internet?

The answer is yes and no. Yes, you have a website. No, your website wasn't prepared to gel with search engine behaviour.

There are millions of websites on the internet and probably hundreds of thousands in the interior design and home improvement niche alone. All those websites are vying for the same visitors you're looking for. How do you set yourself apart? Well, you can't. You can only try.

That's where **Search Engine Optimization, SEO** in short, comes in.

Search engine optimization is a series of techniques used to transform a website from just a collection of webpages and text to a platform that can be recognized by search engines so that they will include it in their search results.

Rather than become just another of the 'hundreds of thousands of home improvement websites on the internet, SEO helps your website become one of the few hundreds that can be featured in its search results. And SEO done right helps your website rise to the top of search results.

And that's how your website can get discovered the next time someone searches for *'affordable interior designers in New Delhi'*.

But how do you start with SEO? SEO is a series of techniques some of which can be done on your webpages (on-page SEO) and some of which have to be done via the 'back end' (off-page SEO). As you may have guessed, some of the techniques are quite technical, so they get really tedious, especially since SEO is a daily continuous process.

One of the reasons I started my company **Searchmetry** was that most of my fellow interior designers were experiencing trouble handling aspects of marketing (particularly thorny ones like search engine optimization) on their own. I had prior experience in working with social media and SEO, so it was a no-brainer.

As of today, Searchmetry handles hundreds of clients from around the world in sprucing up their websites. I included SEO in this book about growing your interior design business because I believe it's necessary more than ever today as the world moves online.

To optimize your website for search engines, you need to know what search engines look for. Some of the most important factors in ranking your website include **the number of links to your website** from other websites (backlinks) and **the keywords used** in your website's content.

Below, I have listed some tips you should follow to get as many backlinks as possible while improving your visibility on the internet.

First, make your business information visible on the internet
Google, social media and other similar service providers have changed the business of online visibility today.

People only have to search for phrases along the lines of *'interior designers in Memphis'* to have interior designers with offices in Memphis show up in search results. It's that easy.

But you have to put in the work. First, you have to offer Google, social media and other similar service providers your business information. In this section, we delve into how to get ahead with each specific service provider.

NB: All of the steps below work only when you have a website for your business (so get one if you don't already).

- **Make your NAP consistent**
  NAP stands for **Name**, **Address** and **Phone Number**. These are the first details about your design business that you make public. It's important to make sure that they are consistent, and that the numbers are similar across Google, Facebook pages, Twitter accounts and more.

Tip: If you're prone to making mistakes, start by writing down your business information on a piece of paper.

- **Set up Your Google My Business (GMB) page**
  Ever searched for a business through Google? If yes, you've probably seen how detailed the results you're offered. Google's 'Google My Business' service is designed to help businesses get their information onto the internet in an organized manner.

  Businesses that get listed have their business name, telephone number, address, working hours and reviews from former visitors easily seen by any potential clients as part of Google's search results. Plus, courtesy of your address, your business gets featured on Google Maps and can then be located by anyone.

  The setup process is not the easiest, so you might need a little help. To spare you the trouble, I have prepared this Google My Business Checklist (www.searchmetry.com/seo-content/uploads/2018/12/Google-My-Business-Profile-Creation-Checklist.pdf) that you can follow point by point to set up your GMB account by yourself.

- **Set up Bing Places for your business**
  Bing, the Microsoft owned search engine, and the in-built search engine for Windows devices also allows for businesses to provide their location information so they can be featured in Bing search results. The process works just like that of Google, so here's a simple Bing Places Checklist (www.searchmetry.com/seo/optimize-bings-places-listing) I created to make life simple for you.

- **Let clients know they can review Your Services on Google**
  The best part about having a business listed on Google My Business is being able to display your reviews for potential clients.

  When you get your business featured on Google My Business, your clients are allowed to leave reviews of your service for future clients to see.

When a client makes a local search, all the related businesses in the area are listed in the search results, along with the cumulated reviews former clients. You can also get a ranking displayed as a series of stars. It's dangerous for your business to be listed without any reviews. You appear unserious, amateurish and sketchy.

So how do you solve this problem? First, let your clients know at the end of every project that they can leave a review of your services online. You will need to generate review links for clients that will enable them to leave reviews on your Google My Business/Bing Places page.

To generate the review link, open the review page and copy the link displayed in the browser. Follow this link (www.searchmetry.com/reviews/create-google-review-links) for a tutorial on how to generate review links for your business.

- ❖ **Claim Your business on Yelp**

  Yelp is an active online review platform, and one of the few that has the power to turn away potential clients in droves. Even worse, clients can give very negative reviews of your service even if you don't have an official page on the platform.

  Yelp's regulations make removal of a negative review very hard too. The best move is to claim your business on the platform by creating an official page that replies to people's comments and averts damage before too much of it is done.

  When you create and own your page on Yelp, the next step is to inform your clients of it and ask them to review your services there. A higher number of positive reviews overshadows any negative reviews you might receive. Good reviews also appear first when clients search for you in any search engine.

  Not all clients will be inclined to leave reviews so, of course, but I have created a guide (see below) that will make it simple for you to convince them to do so.

  At Searchmetry, I handle everything to do with Yelp and the negative comments posted there on behalf of my clients.

  Studies show that you can even turn negative reviews into an advantage for your business. Provided there aren't too many of them and that you can

address the issues raised, visitors may be impressed with your responsiveness.

Here is the [Handling Yelp Reviews Guide](www.searchmetry.com/reviews/yelp-reviews-tips). I have created to help you generate reviews from your clients on Yelp the easy, safe and legal way.

- **Create and build out Your Houzz profile**
  Houzz is a platform designed especially for design professionals; I personally recommend it for your business's visibility. *Architectural Digest* and *CNN* both loved it upon its premiere in 2010, and it's been seeing thousands of users sign up every year.

  The platform allows interior designers, architects and others in the interior design and home improvement world to promote themselves with images of their work, which when clicked on reveal the designer's information.

  Houzz also runs a professional directory of designers and other home improvement professionals that homeowners and potential clients can browse. Naturally, this directory features links to the designer's website, which is good for backlinking and SEO.

  As with every other website and platform online, there are millions of interior designers listed on the platform, so getting a head-start is hard for many designers. The good news is that, with a small target market and location in mind, you can set up quite nicely in no time.

  At the end of the day, it's the photos you share from your past projects that draw eyeballs. Here's a [guide](www.searchmetry.com/social-media/create-houzz-profile) I have created to help you complete your Houzz Profile in a captivating way.

- **Set up Your Facebook Business Page**
  You probably already know how important Facebook is as a means of getting your business greater visibility.

  Facebook, like other social media platforms, is also good for your website's SEO performance. Google's ranking algorithm displays social media pages in search results too.

  To take advantage of what Facebook has to offer, you need an official Facebook page for your business. Ensure that your Facebook page has the same information as your Google My Business page, including your business name, telephone, address and working hours.

With a Facebook page, you get to chat with your potential clients directly when they send you messages(via Facebook Messenger or just by replying to their comments). They can also review your business directly on the page.

The Stories feature is a good opportunity to share what you are working on, as is the Live Feed Feature, which you can use for communicating with potential clients.

Perhaps more importantly, having a Facebook page is a requirement should you ever wish to start running ads on Facebook for your business.

So, what should your Facebook page feature for more conversion? Facebook gives you a few 'insights' on how to improve your page regularly, but I have created a simple guide to take you through the specifics of design, setup, management and promotion. Download my Facebook Page Design Materials guide and Checklist here (www.searchmetry.com/seo-content/uploads/2018/12/Facebook-Page-Creation-Checklist.pdf).

- ❖ **Set up Your Twitter Account**
  In addition to Facebook, Twitter is another platform I recommend taking advantage of. Twitter comes with the rare advantage of introducing your business to wholly new markets, unlike Facebook, Instagram and other platforms that enable engagement mainly between 'friends'.

  Twitter is also perfect for marketing and promotion, thanks to its #hashtags. To take full advantage of Twitter, I have created a guide you can follow when setting up and promoting your account.

  Download this Twitter Page Design Materials guide and Checklist (www.searchmetry.com/seo-content/uploads/2018/12/Twitter-Page-Creation-Checklist.pdf) for free.

- ❖ **Set up Your Pinterest Account**
  I previously mentioned Pinterest as a good addition to your business arsenal of promotional material. Pinterest is also good for your SEO; it gives you and your business more visibility on the internet.

  I have special preference for Pinterest because of its unique design and layout, which makes it ideal for interior designers looking to share and promote their work.

Pinterest's foundational reasoning is that people can crowdsource ideas for things they want to do – kind of what anyone looking to get a house renovation would do. Anyone can own a free Pinterest account but the platform also allows the creation of business accounts. Start by setting up your Pinterest account.

I have created a simple tutorial guide to help you through the setup process. Download the Pinterest Page Design Materials guide and Checklist here (www.searchmetry.com/seo-content/uploads/2018/12/Pinterest-Profile-Creation-Checklist.pdf).

❖ **Set up Your Instagram Account**
From experience, Instagram is one of the best things to happen to interior designers everywhere. The platform has grown in recent years to host tens of millions of active users, some of whom are likely to be your potential clients.

Instagram offers you a platform to showcase your portfolio of finished and upcoming projects, or just share design trends you've found elsewhere.

Most importantly, it gives you the kind of visibility on the internet that results in more backlinks for your website and a proper SERP ranking. Potential clients can access your website from a link you provide in your bio. But you need to set up your Instagram the right way.

This Instagram Profile Checklist (www.searchmetry.com/seo-content/uploads/2018/12/Instagram-Profile-Creation-Checklist.pdf) I've created should guide you through the account setup and profile creation process nicely.

Here's all the links at once.
§Google My Business Checklist - Download (www.searchmetry.com/seo-content/uploads/2018/12/Google-My-Business-Profile-Creation-Checklist.pdf)

§ Bing Places - Read Here (www.searchmetry.com/seo/optimize-bings-places-listing)

§Google My Business - Generate Review Links for Google My Business (www.searchmetry.com/reviews/create-google-review-links)

§ Yelp – Get Reviews on Yelp (www.searchmetry.com/reviews/yelp-reviews-tips)

- § Houzz – [Houzz Profile Setup](www.searchmetry.com/seo-content/uploads/2018/12/Houzz-Profile-Creation-Checklist.pdf)

- § Facebook – [Facebook Page Design Materials guide and Checklist](www.searchmetry.com/seo-content/uploads/2018/12/Facebook-Page-Creation-Checklist.pdf)

- § Twitter – [Twitter Page Design Materials guide and Checklist](www.searchmetry.com/seo-content/uploads/2018/12/Twitter-Page-Creation-Checklist.pdf)

- § Pinterest – [Pinterest Page Design Materials guide and Checklist](www.searchmetry.com/seo-content/uploads/2018/12/Pinterest-Profile-Creation-Checklist.pdf)

- § Instagram – [Instagram Profile Checklist](www.searchmetry.com/seo-content/uploads/2018/12/Instagram-Profile-Creation-Checklist.pdf)

Enable the Ultimate Website Experience

Remember the last time you visited a website on the internet? What did you hate about it? And in the spirit of positivity - what did you like? How was your experience? Chances are that you liked it, if it was a well-designed website.

If it took too long to load, had strange icons you couldn't understand or a menu icon hidden somewhere you couldn't find, the answer is obvious. Those are some of the regular complaints visitors cite about websites on the internet.

Some complaints, such as 'the website does not display properly on my mobile devices and tablets' are real deal breakers. In today's age of unlimited internet-based alternatives, people no longer give sketchy websites any consideration.

Other problems are less general – 'particular page links are hard to find', 'some links don't work', 'images don't load', or 'I always get a 404 error message' – but they are just as damning for your website. And that's not the worst bit.

The real trouble is that unless you're an expert on website design, you may never identify the problems quickly or even at all. A website can scare away visitors while still looking nice. So, what can do?

The only way to give your visitors the ultimate website experience is by tying up every one of your website's loose ends after its development and making sure the ends stay tightened after that.

Here's what to do:
If your website is loading pages slowly, consider;

- **A different host for your website**. I always tell my clients that the cheapest hosting providers aren't always the best. They tend to be oversubscribed, and in the case of a not-too-stellar provider, the result is webpages taking years to load.

  It's smarter to use a better known, highly reviewed hosting provider that may have a higher hosting fee. If your website pages continue being too slow, look for alternative hosting providers.

- **Installing the Google AMP plugin**. Google AMP is a Google backed framework designed to help internet publishers/websites create web pages that load really fast on mobile devices without affecting any existing ad revenue arrangement or existing web experience.

  To start, you get the Google AMP plugin installed on your website. The downside is that installing Google AMP is quite technical in nature (involving schemas and HTML) and tedious because part of the installation process involves manual editing of the website's backend. Still, you can always get someone to do the hard work for you, so don't give up.

To iron out any unusual kinks in your website, go ahead and test it yourself on a regular basis. Ensure that;

- **Your website displays properly on mobile devices and tablets too**. Some websites don't, and if that's your problem, fix it immediately. Google downgrades webpages that don't display well on mobile devices. Get a good developer to fix it if you can't do it on your own.

- **Your website displays properly in all browsers**. While most browsers display each web page more or less the same way, some don't. I have used browsers in which web pages are never responsive, especially on mobile. That can be a total turn off.

Test your website in the major browsers – Google, Bing, Yahoo, Safari, Mozilla and even Opera Mini. The last one is a major culprit as regards unresponsive web pages.

- **All links are working as they should**. There's nothing worse than having a live website whose 'See Demo' or 'Check out our services' or even 'Buy Now' links don't work.

In the case of an interior designer, every link is important, whether it's linking to another website or linking to another page. Test each link out and have it fixed if it appears broken.

- **All icons are easy to see and use.** Whether it's the menu icon or the different social media icons, make sure they are easy to see and use. Menu icons that don't work are literally useless.

And no one wants to feel lost on a new website just because they don't see the basic icons supposed to direct them around. Finally, do have a trained webmaster on standby – unless you're trained in web design.

The backend of a website needs serious attention from time to time (even for seemingly basic things like changing your website's color palette and font), so a good webmaster always comes in handy.

The Point: Having links to and from your website is not enough. Make sure they aren't broken and leading web visitors to 404 error pages by personally testing each of them out and seeing where they lead.

Use Long Tail Keywords

When applying keywords to website content, shorter keywords are normally used, say *'Interior designers in Brooklyn'* or *'nursery renovation'*. For some websites, such short tail keywords are enough for discovery. Not so much for others.

For even better SEO, long tail keywords are recommended. Long tail keywords usually correlate better with what web users might actually search for in their browsers.

So how do you start? By doing the research on the keywords that people are using. Then you can expand them better by making them more specific.

Being more specific means narrowing down your niche and reducing your competition.

Examples of long tail keywords can include *'affordable interior designer based in Brooklyn'* or *'How to spruce up a studio apartment on a budget'*. They're longer and more geographically specific. They are also quite effective for SEO.

The point: Do some research for your keywords and then start integrating longer ones into your content.

Analyze All the Links on Your Website

The links that go in and out of your website are scrutinized by Google and other search engines, such that those websites with more inbound links are ranked higher in search results.

You generate both internal and external links; internal links direct viewers to other pages within the website. You generate external ones when you link to other websites, say when citing something written there or promoting an affiliate product.

When other websites link back to you, they create backlinks. It's these backlinks that excite Google's web crawlers as they browse your website.

But first, you need to make sure that all the links on your website are fully functional. Broken links don't lead anywhere; instead, they drive away visitors.

The Point: Test your website's links regularly to weed out any that are non-functional. There's no reason for links to exist on your website if they don't link to anywhere.

Create Target-specific Content

We already talked about keeping your target audience in mind when designing your website and choosing your niche, but it's even more important to focus on their needs and wants and expectations when creating your content.

I recently visited an insurance company's website and it had one of the most affecting quotes I'd ever read, visibly slapped at the top of the 'life insurance' homepage. It simply read: *"You won't always be there, but we will"*. How touching.

The displayed image of a young, doting woman cuddling her elderly father only made the phrase more emotional and affecting. And just like that, in one short sentence, the message immediately spoke to me.

People with older parents and relatives like me always find ourselves worrying over what will happen to them when we aren't close by or when we're not financially solid.

Insurance is supposed to offer some form of assurance that all will be well, and how better can an insurance company tell me that than by saying it will be there for them even when I am not?

To sum it up, whoever wrote the phrase imagined what the web page visitor was looking for and offered just that. And from my years of experience analyzing what makes websites work, that is the right way to go about it.

When your content directly speaks to a person's needs and questions, they are more likely to stay longer on your website and consider you a valuable web resource. As an interior designer, they are more likely to check out your 'Portfolio' web page.

(In this scenario, content is anything from the copy on each webpage to the blog posts that you publish, should you choose to have a blog).

But how do you make content target specific? First, you identify what your potential client might be looking for. For an interior designer, they can be searching for anything from interior designers in their area to DIY ideas for redesigning their bedrooms.

Imagine everything from *'affordable interior designers in Raleigh'* and *'how to renovate a kitchen'* to *'do I need an interior designer?'* Then see if you can answer those questions.

Additionally, go back to the sample customers you created for your target market (**see chapters 5**) and identify what they might need.

If you're targeting male bachelors with a taste for clean, urban style, you've got to imagine what they'd like to see and what they'd need. There's no way their content would be similar to the kind another designer will create for his married couple audience.

Geographical consideration is equally important. Your target audience must have a specific location, maybe a city or a country, and your content must reflect that. Trends and designs may appear universal but they aren't always.

Some aspects of interior design speak to certain regions more than others. Ever wondered why a design studio offering interior design services to residential homes in India would have a smiling middle-aged Indian matriarch smiling in her neatly done living room as its hero image?

Because that's one way to make a client feel like they are in the right place. That's how you localize content. A *sari* clad matriarch definitely wouldn't do for a US based design firm.

I have found that most designers prefer to speak to a wider audience with more generic content, but that isn't a smart move considering you're looking to make your design business grow twofold, not just boost your online presence.

A smaller, better targeted audience as we discussed in earlier chapters is the sweet spot while marketing your design business. And when you're dealing with smaller, niche markets, you have to create the specific answers to the specific queries and needs they have (and probably won't find anywhere else).

That's how your website becomes linked to, quoted and shared, all of which are tremendous boosters for your SEO performance.

The Point: Think about what your ideal client would be looking for/asking/needing when they visit your website. Design your website and fill it with content that answers your client's questions.

Take Advantage of Categories and Tags

At the end of blog posts on most websites today, you will see a section for tags and categories related to that blog post. It's not just another eye-popping web feature. Tags and categories are two resources I always recommend.

The power of categorizing and tagging is that it makes site navigation a breeze for your clients, especially when they are looking for specific content not directly listed on your website.

Imagine how tedious it would be to manually categorize all of your blog posts under the tags *'affordable*, *'design'*, *'Architectural Digest'* or *'tools'*, or categories as wide as *'home renovation'*, *'Pinterest finds'* or *'interior designer'*.

Some posts would appear in more than one category, and you'd have to read through each to ascertain that. You'd waste a lot of valuable time and probably never get done.

Categorizing and tagging makes automatic the usually tedious job of putting all blog posts concerning *'bathroom tiles'* together so you don't have to. All you have to do is add tags and categorize each blog post right after writing it.

WordPress makes it easy as does Wix. Visitors looking for specific information on a particular topic won't have to scroll through all your blog posts since 2005 to get what they want.

If the topic is *'bathroom tiles'*, all they'll have to is look for tags connected to the topic, such as *'bathrooms'*, *'bathroom renovation'* or *'tile ideas'*. Clicking on one tag opens all the articles connected to the topic at once. The same applies to categories. Additionally, tags and categories are good for ranking in search engine results.

The Point: You need categories and tags. Don't overlook them when creating your content.

Optimize All the Photos on Your Website

Even the photos you use on your website help directly with the website's SEO and rankings in search results. Photographs are an integral part of any interior designer's website; photos of past projects, photos of you and your team at work, and everything else.

But rather than just dropping them onto your website, you need to make them work for you. Enter optimization. SEO experts suggest that optimizing your website's images starts with choosing the right file name for each image.

In other words, an image of a revamped living room should be labelled as '*remodeled-living-room.jpg*', not '*abdc2.jpg*'. The other ways to optimize the images on your website for SEO are;

§**Making them responsive**. Images need to be as responsive as web pages for a proper viewing experience on various device screens.

§**Captioning them right**. Not every image needs to be captioned, but those that do should be captioned right, in the sense of the image naming process mentioned earlier.

§**Adding alt text/alt tag to every image**. Alt text is what is displayed in case an image does not load, and is particularly good for SEO.

§**Resizing images** to the actual size you want visitors to see. Large, high quality images take longer to load, so you need to resize them to a medium size that doesn't slow down your page loading speed.

§**Compressing them** before use to smaller sizes without affecting quality. Use services like *Kraken.io* and *PunyPNG* to compress.

§**Choose the right format for your images**. PNG is Google's recommended image format because it keeps the smallest details even at high resolution, but JPEG works just fine too.

§**Add images to your XML Sitemaps**. This is a bit more technical than all the other steps but it's just as necessary. Google scans a webpage for minute details of information before ranking it in search results, so sitemaps are a good way to make the process easy.

Start Guest Posting and Contributing Content

In an earlier section, I explained that Google and other search engines place immense weight on the number of times other sites link back to your website, and that their number and quality directly determine how high your website appears in search results. These links are known as backlinks.

Getting such links is a major way of boosting your design website's SEO. And while there are countless methods of getting these backlinks, some legal and others not, one that works pretty well is *guest posting*.

Guest posting involves creating content in your area of expertise for a website or platform others than yours. The idea is to offer value to readers on other platforms while marketing yourself as an expert at what you do, i.e. *a win-win*.

Most websites offer a linkback to your website at the end of the guest post you've created for them, hence the backlinks we talked about earlier. The more backlinks you get from trusty (or, as Google calls them, 'high authority') websites, the higher your website's ranking will go in search results.

That explains why online platforms such as *Forbes* and *Entrepreneur* have a large percentage of guest content today, and why getting published with them is a big deal. For interior designers, authority websites such as *Houzz* and *Apartment Therapy* are more ideal.

To be seen by your local target audience, your choice of platform matters. It must be one that your target customer would definitely read. There's no need to get worked up over getting published in *Architectural Digest* if your ideal audience and target market is local to Mumbai and reads *Mumbai Mirror* or *Mid-Day*.

To start guest posting, here's a list (www.searchmetry.com/seo/list-of-30-quality-blogs-that-accept-guest-posts) I've curated of websites and platforms in the home improvement and interior space niche that accept guest posts. Some pay for each post and others don't.

The point: Look for websites and other platforms in the interior design niche that you can contribute to. Read through their content and see if it offers value for your target audience.

Do your research to see if the publication speaks to your target audience. Look for the platform's contacts and reach out to them to make a formal request. Ideally, start by reading their guest posting guidelines.

When you get the gig, do your best to offer value. Most websites look for guest posts on issues that haven't been covered yet.

Podcasts and Other Media Appearances

Earlier on, I introduced podcasts as a good way of marketing your interior design business. Their smaller, targeted audiences are quite good for businesses looking for select, targeted customers and those looking to draw immediate attention to a new service or product.

Even when working to get good SEO, podcasts are a smart option. Not only do they spread your authority across the internet, but they also offer an opportunity for backlinks to your website. How?

Podcasts have websites, and when you are featured on the podcast you get an opportunity to market your business on it by offering a link to your own website. Get featured on more podcasts and you will build a steady stream of trustworthy websites linking to yours.

Google rewards you nicely for that with a good ranking in search results. Of course, directing a podcast's listeners to your website for a particular service or promotion also works wonders traffic-wise.

And while the listeners may not always be in your immediate location, it still introduces you to a new audience that can take future interest in your services.

How does one get started? It's easy. You can search online for popular podcasts in the interior design and home improvement niche. You can also use your phone's podcast app (download one if you don't have it) to discover podcasts in your intended category.

Listen to each podcast to gauge how it suits your target audiences. When you like a particular podcast, check out it's website, get it contacts and shoot them an email.

Starting your own podcast or web show: If you are an ardent podcast fan already, I am sure that you have already considered creating your own podcast to serve your business's marketing needs.

I believe this is a good idea, especially if you are starting a video podcast, but it's one you need to consider with caution. While a podcast of your own is a wonderful marketing plan, podcasts are tedious to start and maintain.

You might never find enough time for it —quite a few designers have intimated to me in the past that they couldn't even manage their own websites, let alone a podcast – and it will take up more than an hour everyday of your time.

This is not to discourage you though. If you have the time and resources, go ahead and start your own podcast.

And when you do, make sure you offer value, speak directly to your target audience with specific topics and make your podcast work for your business as regards SEO. You can still appear on other podcasts as a guest too, so it's a win-win situation.

The point: Podcasts are a good option for both SEO and marketing your business. Search for those that your ideal audience would listen to and ask them to feature you.

Plus, when looking out for podcasts, consider both audio and video podcasts. Many of my former clients used to skip video until it was too late.

The Ranking Process

After you have done your fair share of SEO on your business's website, the next thing to wait for is the change in search result ranking. This is the ultimate result to work for, and whatever you get is determined by how much work you put in.

So, how long does it take for your website to appear on the first and second page of the search results, you might ask? The answer is anything from few weeks to a few months.

There are millions of active websites on the internet, and a quarter of that number is directly part of or related to the interior design, architecture and home improvement niche.

That's just a quick breakdown of the amount of competition you face when ranking, assuming all the other websites are applying proper SEO as well.

Ultimately, ranking takes time. Google's algorithm (and all the other search engines') is a company secret and works in its own way. It's never stable either – last month's exact criteria for ranking high may have changed by next week's. It still follows certain guidelines so web publishers aren't left hanging.

According to experts on SEO and ranking, the algorithm uses bots that crawl every website on the internet to identify keywords that match with what a user has requested for in the browser.

The websites that are better optimized and have better matching keywords rank higher than others. This whole process may take a while to bear fruit and the results may not show immediately after you implement your SEO processes. But the good news is that search engines always identify well optimized websites in the end.

The point: As you might have noticed, optimizing a website for better ranking in search results is no easy task. The fact that it's something you need to keep working on as long as you intend to keep your website online just makes the situation bleaker. But you need to have your website properly optimized, and you can't take shortcuts.

I always recommend that my clients hire someone to handle this part of their business marketing. It's better knowing you have someone you can trust handling the digital marketing side of things so you can concentrate on what you love and what you're trained to do – designing.

Searchmetry, my company, offers Search engine optimization (SEO) services specifically for interior designer and architects.

My own background as an interior design marketer makes me very understanding of the specific needs of different interior design businesses.

I have had the pleasure of collaborating with over a 100 design businesses across the US and India and seeing the results speak for themselves. If you need to see your interior design business website jump from obscurity to first page visibility, I am the right person to contact.

Find me here (www.searchmetry.com/contact) and tell me how your website is doing.

✽ CHAPTER TAKEAWAYS ✽

- ✓ As long as you have a website on the internet, you will need to optimise it with SEO. Otherwise, nobody but you will ever see it.

- ✓ Never forget the power of backlinks from authoritative websites on the internet in helping boost your website's visibility. Get as many backlinks as possible but remember to avoid getting any from spammy websites.

- ✓ Podcasts, much like websites, are a good way to get backlinks to your website. You also get to meet new audiences who could become clients.

- ✓ You can always start your own podcast. No big deal.

- ✓ Visitors to your website need to have a full, seamless experience navigating its pages, and that means it should be quick to load, have active links and have easy-to-see-and-use icons.

- ✓ Always make sure the content you produce for your website and other platforms is relevant to your target audience. If it isn't, don't bother with it.

CHAPTER 10:

Ending Notes

As we near the end of the book, let me recapitulate the 6 most important takeaways (or lessons) for you. These are the things that you simply must embed into your business promotion strategy. These are the things you must ensure your graphic designer or social media manager, should you hire them, follow.

Most of my clients have had only positive things to say about the advice I give them - and it is the same advice that I have collated in this book. So you can safely assume that what I have to say works and will guide you in the right direction.

***

Lesson 1:
Identify Your Target Audience from the Beginning

There is no bigger determinant for your success as an interior designer than identifying the market you want to work for from the very start.

There are many successful interior designers today that work for every type of client, but as an up and coming business, concentrating a specific market is the best start.

We discussed the upsides of identifying your target market in earlier chapters. Once you select a target market, everything to do with your interior design business, including changes to your logo, portfolio and marketing strategy will have to be attuned to this target market's interests.

To understand the needs and interests of your target markets, you need to study them first.

I explained in an earlier chapter that you have to look into what they like and what they don't, plus other smaller details such as what they read and what they look for on the internet. That way, you can create content and adverts that they will be sure to find – and understand.

***

Lesson 2:
Grow Your Authority and Make it Public

People love dealing with experts. They love the unspoken guarantee expertise gives them of how good the services offered will be. So, go ahead. Do your research. Know your facts and update them regularly. Do the necessary reading. Be available for quotes and interviews.

Grow your authority on interior design and then make it public. Write guest posts on websites and columns in your local paper, appear on podcasts, make web shows, do anything that introduces you as an authoritative individual to new audiences.

Your contact book will thank you.

***

Lesson 3:
See What's Working for Other Interior Designers

We discussed competitive analysis in an earlier chapter, and I can't overstate how important it is. Every company does their version of competitive analysis, so you won't be doing anything wrong.

> **Competitive analysis gets you one step further. It shows you what's working and what's not.**

So, go deeper and find out how other designers are getting their clients. Discover their strengths and weaknesses. Think how you can counter their strengths while avoiding their mistakes and maybe capitalizing on their weaknesses. Use your results to strategize your future marketing endeavours.

***

Lesson 4:
Make Use of Social Media and Platforms such as Houzz

The power of social media and its viral feature (maybe even as you read this something is 'going viral' on the internet) cannot be understated, especially for interior designers today. Platforms such as Instagram and Pinterest are leading the way but you can't forget Facebook and Twitter for their uniqueness.

Take advantage of these platforms. They are a good source of exposure for your projects, the kind of exposure that leads to new clients.

You can't let industry-specific platforms such as Houzz slip out of your fingers either, but you have to navigate them smartly too to avoid being part of the group that never gets noticed on the platform.

NB: If you aren't very well versed with the intricacies of social media, you might want to hire someone to help you.

Social media managers are good additions to teams, but only hire one when you're certain you're going to go big on social media.

***

Lesson 5:
Networking is Key

There is a reason the most introverted people still go to parties. It's almost never for the food or the lights or the dancing, but for the networking possibilities parties present. Not every interior designer is an introvert – I know many that turn the word on its head – but you might be one.

And even if you indeed are the kind that prefers quiet isolation over loud public environments, you'll still need to get out and mingle from time to time. But hold up: am not saying that you must accept every party invitation or buy your way into every party in town.

You must identify an occasion or event for its value before getting a ticket. In other words, who'll be there? Are they vital contacts for your business?

Industry events are a good start. And when you get in there, don't push your business down people's throats. Engage in meaningful conversation and only talk about your business when the time is right.

Remember to be able to pitch your business-like a pro would; you have to pitch it in a way that makes your design business appear like a valuable partner to whoever you're pitching to.

The power of networking is that even if your ideal client doesn't buy your services, they might recommend you to someone else. You don't want to miss out on that.

***

Lesson 6:
Create Stunning Portfolios

This should be easy. But it never is. You might, rather unfortunately, be one of those designers who randomly puts photos together and calls it a day, or, *fortunately*, one of those that don't. A stunning portfolio is your way into people's minds – especially potential clients.

Portfolios show your experience, your range, your design mind, your techniques and your uniqueness. A good portfolio will get a more expensive or more obscure designer hired instead of the obvious choice. That's how instrumental it is.

ABOUT THE AUTHOR

I am Anita Sharma, an interior design marketing consultant based in Kolkata. I have had stints in various forms of marketing over the years, of late concentrating on marketing for interior designers as a way of helping fellow designers work through the confusion of the internet and its incessant and ever changing demands.

As a young marketer I quickly realised that there were so many opportunities for businesses to market themselves and grow, especially on the internet. My initial attempts to help interior designers take advantage of this opportunity weren't so successful.

Over time, however I have been able to help more and more designers reshape their marketing strategies in response to the changing landscape and with increasingly positive results.

I feel honoured in knowing that I have helped people with their interior design businesses, and that I have had a small part to play in many a success story over the years. With this book, I hope to take you one step further towards the success that you deserve.

If you need a one-to-one consultation with me for your interior design business, I am available for you. All you need to do is to book a consultation (www.searchmetry.com/consult) with me. Rest assured, I will get in touch with you as soon as possible.

I still hope you will be inspired to keep at it until your interior design business gets to the level you've always wanted.

***